The Fifth Dimension

The present volume is one of a sequence of books by the same author on the application of the Ancient Wisdom to modern living :

THE FIFTH DIMENSION

THE INITIATION OF THE WORLD

THE FINDING OF THE THIRD EYE

WISDOM IN PRACTICE

THE SECRET OF THE ATOMIC AGE

WHEN HUMANITY COMES OF AGE

(Individual and World Fulfilment)

The author has drawn upon so many sources for this book that it is impossible to enumerate them especially as she has accepted no postulate from one source only. She would like here to express her heartfelt thanks and appreciation to all who have helped to make this book possible.

Contents

Contents

Part III
CONTEMPLATION—THE ORACLE SPEAKS

Part IV
DEDICATION

Preface

There are many today who are trying to look at the world with clear eyes. To them it seems as if civilisation is at the cross-roads—or even that it has become trapped in a blind alley.

There seems to be complete congestion between the forces of tyranny and those who are minded for liberty and peace. Although the existence of these dual streams is obvious, they yet seem so mixed and criss-crossed that they can only create chaos. Perhaps the age-long practice of compromise has produced a tapestry of civilisation in which the good and bad threads are so inextricably interwoven that it would be hopeless to try and clarify them and introduce order and integrity into the pattern.

Today men are spending most of their substance on material for mutual slaughter. In such a way are the first two thousand years of the Christian era drawing to a close.

The world presents a panorama in which progress and barbarism, organisation and chaos, brilliance and stupidity, are accepted with a kind of conditioned blindness, a lack of values which renders non-existent the 'will of the people'. Humanity seems sunk to the neck in a quagmire of muddle through energetic ineffectiveness. Energy is spent in producing marvellous inventions, and ineffectiveness is the result of the way in which these inventions are used.

What has gone wrong? Is there true cause for hope or for

despair? Is it possible to read the riddle of human evolution, to discover the clue to future progress, and to find the means by which humanity can be set free from the present apparent deadlock? For civilisation has reached an impasse involving economics, health, morality and self-knowledge. Is there any way of piercing the fog of surface happenings, and of understanding the real trend and significance of events?

In my first two books we studied life as presented to us by the great minds of all times, including the present epoch. We outlined the world-wide science by means of which the greatest discoverers and prophets in history have acquired their wisdom and knowledge—the science of Meditation. In Egypt, in Babylonia, in China, in Tibet, in India—in every great culture, we find Meditation producing the basis of morality and of law, whether through the oracle, the guru, the high priest, a Buddha, a Pythagoras, and finally, a Christ. All taught that human beings contain a channel within themselves which, when developed, connects them directly with the Universal Mind, the Universal Love and the Universal Purpose.

The Buddha fasted under the Bod Tree, until His Meditation opened His channel to 'Nirvana'.

Christ fasted forty days in the desert, until His Meditation inspired Him to His task. He said: 'Only by prayer and fasting shall ye come unto Me.'

Pythagoras, of the Greek Golden Age, would not accept pupils until they had kept silence for a definite number of years.

But, alas, after that, the age of barbarism set in, and these wonderful teachings were forgotten.

It seems very strange, surely, that now, when there is talk of the coming of a New Age of enlightenment, the world-wide violence and disruption everywhere is coupled with a new interest in Meditation amongst the people themselves, amongst the new young arrivals of this generation around the globe.

For some time now there seems to have been an instinctive recognition that a new and better world civilisation can only emerge after the chrysalis of tradition, habit and heredity has been cracked open and burst asunder, allowing escape into the light of freedom and the nakedness of the unconditioned.

Such a transition necessitates destruction of the old forms, both of thought and action. It produces revolutionary and experimental attitudes which find their first expression in the fine arts, which are always prophetical. We have watched this happen, first in the realm of music, then of literature, and then of art and sculpture—James Joyce, Gertrude Stein, Picasso.

In their access of rebellion against outworn ways, these pioneers produced works whose effort has been to break apart and disrupt habitual mental ruts and attitudes, and to introduce the unexpected, the unnatural, the meaningless. Instinctively they prepare the way for something which has to come, something utterly new and different—although they do not yet know what that will be. Nevertheless, several decades of such inspiration has indeed found its mark in the consciousness of the people. It has gate-crashed the apathy of their conditioning, and aroused them to more mature need for realisation and self-determination.

So the new awakening urges have begun to express themselves outwardly, beginning of course in physical resistance against the old traditions and authorities. This preliminary stage of destruction of the outworn is painful, even terrifying, to the unperceptive. But already there are signs of the second stage, the rebuilding towards new values and along experimental lines, the desire to take responsibility in planning and in action.

Much of this has been rehearsed before in history, with the rise and fall of many civilisations. But today there are two new differences. Firstly, the revolution is world wide; secondly, although all races and classes are taking part, it is led by the *youth* of all nations. They seem to forgo youth's careless rapture and to suffer discomfort, danger, and disruption and to give service and even thought to the rebuilding and re-modelling of social and educational conditions.

It is true that rebellion brings with it elements of violence, of despair and of distortion—it always has. Thus, today's young people, in their determination to enlarge their awareness of hidden potentials, first take to drugs (the self-destructive angle) and later to the more constructive and radical practice of Meditation.

Here they are faced with much danger. For who is qualified to teach them, in ways suitable to this day and age, and comprehensible to the utterly untrained? Is their legitimate aspiration to be betrayed, by half truths, wrong emphasis, vagueness or even dangerous practices? As a world-wide and age-old practice, Meditation has many facets, many systems, and possibly as many distortions as have infiltrated most of our great religions. How are we going to find our way to the underlying truths, if any, and will it be worth our while? For it is claimed that by meditation and through meditation only, spiritual growth and ultimate knowledge, wisdom and achievement are possible—and that this achievement is unimaginably glorious.

It therefore seems essential that we should consider, first of all, how much truth there is in the claims made for Meditation; what exactly happens or develops in the student; and what is the biological and physical activity which takes place. Further, it will be well to outline the whole practice of balanced living which is included in this science; the stages of development which ensue, and the phenomena which lead step by step to the ultimate fulfilment and achievement.

After we have made this exploration of the purpose of Meditation and its techniques, we will, together, do an experiment. We will make a demonstration of an actual Meditation—a constructive train of thought—which will build up into new discoveries without the use of books or of any outside help. We will choose a subject about which we are likely to know *nothing*! Step by step we will construct our 'channel' to the Universal Mind, and we will see how much knowledge, new to us, we can draw down through it.

Thus we will find out what Meditation is, and how it works within the human being; which are its techniques most suited to ourselves; and to what results we can look forward. Our purpose in this experiment will be to make an approach to an understanding of the divine plan of evolution and progress (if there is one) so that we might intelligently and successfully collaborate with it, thus bringing an entirely new and exciting element into our lives.

During the time of this experiment and the writing of this book, we will open no other volume, nor use any visible source of information whatsoever. The memory of our former studies,[1] coupled with energetic thinking, will suffice for us.

Individual thinking is a rare and difficult function with most of us. Some of us may feel ill-disposed to follow through with the rather scientific beginnings of our research. Those who skip that portion of the work may arrive at the end saying 'Astonishing! Interesting! But one cannot possibly know whether there is any truth in it'! Those who enter seriously into the spirit of the experiment will, on the other hand, be likely to discover even more than we may capture in these pages!

SUGGESTED ADDITIONAL READING

Concentration and Meditation, Christmas Humphreys, London, Stuart and Watkins
Food Combining Made Easy, Herbert Shelton's Health School, San Antonio, Texas, U.S.A.
Letters on Occult Meditation, Alice A. Bailey, London, Lucis Trust
The Spirit of Zen, Alan W. Watts, London, John Murray

[1] *The Finding of the Third Eye* and *The Initiation of the World.*

Introduction: What is Meditation?

What is Meditation? Is it something vague? Is it in any way practical? Could it be called scientific?—deeply scientific? perhaps the most scientific activity in existence? What is its history? What are said to be the results of its practice? What kind of people have been and are, its exponents? Has it a biological or physical function? Has it definite effects on psychological activities? Does it affect energy output? How does it compare with the taking of drugs?

Is Meditation really connected with the Pituitary body and the Pineal gland, and other brain organs, and if so how can we prove it? To what extent can we experiment with it ourselves? Why was it, in various forms, considered to be the essential foundation for national Government in ancient civilisations?

By the time we have considered all these questions we will know whether the practice of Meditation and all that it includes is really what we are after in order to build a new and wonderful life for ourselves, independently of all circumstances.

The practice of Meditation has been, and should be, only part (albeit the most important part) of a complete way of life designed to bring development and maturity, firstly in the invisible components of the mind, secondly in the visible brain growth, and thirdly in the orientation and control of action. There is such a wealth of literature, sometimes, alas, contradictory, on this age-old science, that a clear-cut summary is needed for so many of us who have, perhaps, but little time in which to obtain a hold of the subject.

It is rather the same as the search for the ideal diet. We are confronted with a mass of literature, some of which contradicts the other quite wildly. This is because, of course, everyone is at different stages of need and understanding. However, during my own search amongst the masses of diet books, I finally came across quite a tiny volume which explained exactly what happened during digestion, and according to what one had eaten. This helped me more than any before, because I could now visualise the actual proven processes, and realise what happened with each combination eaten, under different circumstances and conditions. This analysis gave me a working basis on which to form my own conclusions and decisions, and build up a programme to suit my particular stage and projects.

Surely the same should be written regarding Meditation, which is, after all, a process of choice, combination, assimilation, digestion, elimination, rebuilding and use in activity.

We might therefore begin by ascertaining the *mental* organs of intellectual digestion, and their reactions to choice, combination of ideas, 'food for thought', digestion, subsequent nourishment, good or bad, and successful elimination of the unwanted! We must find out whether such mental organs exist.

Science has taught us that in the last analysis all is energy, and that the most powerful and actual activities are those we cannot see. It appears that the visible is really only a kind of sheath and focal point for the basic invisible activity. An instance of this is the vast power focused through an atom, and the invisible genius at work within a cell.

Therefore in the study of any subject we have to take into account two of its parts, the visible and the invisible.

However, a fuller analysis can prove that there are really three parts—*1* the so-called solid part, presenting to us the sheath and form which isolates its activities; *2* the electrical counterpart, whose existence can be proved and contacted through a study of radiations, and which is able to manipulate the solid matter (as an instance of this we can refer to certain types of healing); and *3* the truly invisible authority back of it all, that mysterious 'I' which is veiled in so many complexities. Are we able to locate our 'I' and examine it?

For instance, what part of *you* is it that has decided to read this book, and is activated by a desire for progress and for knowledge? There is another part of *you* which resists this effort, which is lazy, which is pleasure-seeking—which is surely in opposition? So we begin right away with two parts, that which wants to achieve something and that which is against it. Then you will agree that there is a third part—the conditioned part, which makes one want to do only what is expected of one. This may be in direct opposition to the other two.

We can soon ascertain that the human temperament is usually divided into at least three parts; and any new crisis, book or circumstance may at once create a fourth part. You will immediately see that these divisions, all pulling against one another, are each using up energy, and thus not only diminishing the total energy available for any one act or thought, but actually causing energies to collide and devour each other.

Thus, one's potential energy inheritance is spoilt, diffused, scattered or inhibited from the very start. At the earliest age one is taught 'You must not' do this, think that, etc. It is a world of *don'ts* which cause one to start putting the brakes on one's natural exuberance, curiosity and 'will-to-do'. As a rule one is given no logical reasons for these 'don'ts'. Our self-repression is obliged to be unquestioning, and influenced by fear of reprisals. We crush down our real desires to know, to do and to experience, and we have no sound reasons for the patterns into which we are being moulded.

A part of us is perhaps content to have our thinking and organising done for us, whilst another part of us is in deep rebellion, either conscious or subconscious—or even super-conscious.

All this obviously builds within us a situation of criss-cross energies, desires, resentments, frustrations and even apathies, which eventually produce chaos in our orientation, our realisation and our state of identity. We have allowed this whole condition within ourselves to be enclosed, beaten together and moulded into the required social pattern like a piece of dough for bread-making!

Our personalities are therefore like lumps of dough wherein all the ingredients are held prisoner in inextricable and un-congenial congestion. When people speak to us our replies pop out automatically, mostly habitual reflexes without thought (a good example is our famous weather exchanges!). If we are asked an unwonted question we suffer actual mental pain at the prospect of having to think out an answer. We usually cannot do it, but trot out whatever attitudes we have adopted from our spasmodic reading or listening habits.

If this is a true picture of some of us, is not such a situation really death in life? and is it not a horrible result of genera-tions of a blind following of the line of least resistance—letting the other fellow do our thinking for us? Is this not a tragic state of affairs when one considers that it is possible that any one of us may have a potentially remarkable mind, an amazing will-power, unlimited energy, and an inner fountain of know-ledge and wisdom, if only he could break out of the terrible prison of conditioning described above?

Certainly this will need a dynamic first effort, but it will mean the difference between being a half-dead puppet, and a living, adventuring, influential individual.

How much does such a change and such an adventure mean to us? Can we make sufficient effort? And what effort would that have to be?

The way to such achievement has been patiently developed and demonstrated by certain wise people throughout history. It has been built around the science which we now know as Meditation. This science has existed in all systems or religions planned for the essential development of man. In ancient Egypt the motto of this science was 'MAN KNOW THY-SELF'. The belief was that people can only reach real success and fulfilment by first of all learning exactly what human beings are, how they are made, their relationship with the rest of nature, the steps by which they can approach spiritual awakening; and finally what they have to look forward to after death.

As you see, the ancient Egyptians purported to know far more about the human situation than we would assume at this day and age. But did they know? and has this knowledge been lost? We find that the same kind of knowledge existed in Tibet, and that in China vast Tômes and Archives on such subjects were preserved at the Emperor's Court, to which he was liable to add his own learned Commentaries. In India any parents would willingly give up their small son if he were selected by the sages for vocational training in such self-development.

One of the names for such a way of life was YOGA, a system planned to unite the human personality with its divine source, or dynamic potency. Yoga embraced many branches, and Meditation was a fundamental part of the training. In those early days people were far more leisured than we are today, and could often devote their whole lives to such development. In the West, the monks and nuns developed such types of training in their own ways.

However, human failings gradually built up such conditions of luxury, oppression, warfare, exploitation and ignorance, that the long dark ages of superstition and materialism set in, and obliterated the awareness of the existence of spiritual wisdom, which earlier had been innate in all peoples. Thus the human spirit became separated from its own heritage and glory, and an inner despair and disorientation destroyed its natural integrity. By the time the Buddha came, he had to rediscover the essential spiritual techniques, including Meditation. And Christ, after He had been beautifully trained by the Essenes and others, was faced with a public of immature primitive ignorance, very different to conditions which had been obtained in earlier civilisations.

The so-called Dark Ages had set in. Now, after two thousand years, we are witnessing the chaos and world-wide distress which are the results of neglecting and compromising with the noble sciences of fulfilment so generously bequeathed to man.

Things have reached such a pass that either mankind will collapse utterly into moral self-destruction, or a vigorous reaction will arouse the will to regenerate and rebuild before it is too late. When such a reaction comes it must be taken at its flood tide, or the opportunity will be lost. There must be available concise and trustworthy information as to the ways and means of awakening the true self and the intrinsic power for good which lies waiting within humanity.

It is vital that such information is ready to hand, so that man can have an exact picture of what he can achieve, and how he can produce in himself an instrument of service and of salvation on this striving, struggling planet.

Let us, therefore, build up a blue-print of the situation within ourselves, and the technique with which we can master it.

PART I

What is Meditation?

I

The Miracle of Man

Our adventure must begin by a preliminary look at that which we are going to tackle. What potential order lies beneath the chaos which now represents our personalities? We will have to start with a simple analysis of the human being's equipment, from the angle of his power to direct his own capacities and destiny.

The body of man and its component parts are truly a collection of unbelievable miracles, which function, when in good health, so smoothly that one is usually unaware of their existence (even if the functioning is either one-horsepower or inhibited by the conditions cited above). Nevertheless, even the slightest study of ordinary anatomy will show up the astounding cleverness of design which lies behind the body's movements and capacities.

From the contemplation of the outer physical form, we can pass on to a consideration of the geniuses within that form which control metabolism and all other functions—namely the endocrine glands. They say 'A man is what his glands are'! There are seven major endocrine glands, each one embracing its special variety of activities, which include the production of intricate and specific juices, hormones, and types of energy, for definite purposes and functions within the body.

Any one of these glands is a marvel of ingenuity and of competence, impossible of conception to the average man in whose body they exist. Each gland appears to be ruled by its own genius, and to be empowered by an especial flow of radiations and energies passing through it. From where do they come? By whom are these ruling glands themselves ruled? Here we pass from all that which is well known to orthodox medicine, to the sphere which is still awaiting discovery. It is being realised that this subtle invisible sphere is able to affect the so-called physical or solid sphere; and that it is in reality the causative factor behind every outer gland; a kind of dynamo, a receiver of intelligent impulses; a vibrating, radiating centre which controls and feeds not only its gland but the bodily organs which are associated with that gland.

We have to admit that in all ancient Wisdom literature these dynamos were seen by 'extra sight' (the clairvoyants of those days). They were described and recognised as the *real* superphysical organs of the body. They were known as the 'chakras' in the Eastern philosophies, and as the 'etheric centres' in later Western metaphysics. They were the channels for radiatory forces which played into the endocrine glands, nourished them and controlled their activities. These invisible centres behind the glands inhabit a medium or stratum between solid and electrical manifestation which has been known as the 'ether'. This mysterious substance is said to be still of physical nature, but at a much finer rate of vibration which enables it to act as a framework through which certain building forces can congeal their conceptions into 'solid' matter.

From here we can once again ask: If the glands are controlled by these mysterious invisible 'centres', who controls *them*? It appears that, to a certain extent, it is the man himself, whose intricate nature affects the development of his own glands. He starts off, of course, with an inherited situation, after which he is subjected to social conditioning and environment, to diet, climate, and to his own response to all these.

Before long he has in this way developed his own unique pattern where his glands are concerned. By repressions and tensions he can inhibit the flow of blood and of energy to any of his glands. Or by undue emphasis on any bodily function he can build up an abnormal condition. When he tenses up in anxiety or repulsion, he is doing so by means of electrical impulses which, using the medium of the ether, play through his nervous system. His mind can function all over his body like a flash of lightning, using the body's ether counterpart along which to travel. The mind can project a thought outside the body to a far distance, also using the ether as a medium.

All this is known, and it is not really the subject of this book. But we must build up an elementary picture of ourselves as we are made, and as we function, in order to visualise what is happening when we try to meditate. Visualisation gives control, and we will need a great measure of control.

The seven major endocrine glands are set near to the spinal column, and work closely with its intricate network of nerves.

The gland at the base of the spine controls the life-impulse, the 'will-to-survive'. It is connected with the adrenal glands, the glands of 'fight and fright', who respond quickly to any emergency.

A little way up the spine we find the sacral centre, the gonads, which run the sex life, the will to create on the physical plane. They are linked with the Thyroid gland which runs a higher type of creative faculty.

Moving further up the spine we come to the Solar Plexus, run by a powerful gland and centre. It has been called the Lower Brain. It takes care of man's 'animal' nature.

Further up still, we come to the sphere of the heart and lungs, whose ruler is the Thymus gland. This gland is usually recessional, because of the under-developed condition of man.

Above the heart centre we come to the sphere of the throat and voice. This is run by the Thyroid gland, with its interesting partnership with the little Parathyroid bodies. In the throat centre we have the potential basis for human creativity as differentiated from the animals, who share in all the glandular conditions so far mentioned.

When the Thymus centre functions again, the heart also will become a thinking creative medium, but with most people this lies in the far future.

We now leave the spine, and rising up into the head we will find the remaining endocrine glands. We know, of course, of the existence of the Pineal gland and the Pituitary body, of the Carotid gland, and of the medulla oblongata.

But the situation in the human head presents us with a new picture. The human brain has a fundamental resemblance to the human embryo or foetus. It presents the component parts of a bodily form, with the repeat of the endocrine glandular pattern in miniature. The little form is hermaphrodite. The Pineal and Pituitary represent the male and female elements, whilst there are two perfectly-formed little breasts, known as the mammary glands. It is taught that the prototype of the new human embryo takes shape first in the head, and that the baby's little body grows as an extrusion or externalisation of the inner brain form; and that the glandular entity within the skull builds and runs its outer extension, the complete human being, just as a governor may control his domain. This occurs successfully or otherwise according to the varying state of the glands within both head and body, and the amount of co-operation and of sharing of energy which exists between them.

Here we are coming to the crux of our subject. The genius which exists within each endocrine gland is inclined to appropriate power, to try if possible to rule not only its environment but its host, the total personality. It can build up such a usurping of power through the energies which it draws from the human mind. For instance, if the human mind focuses on the pleasure of drinking alcohol, it will send so much energy to the seat of this pleasure, the genius of the digestive glands, that he will usurp power, and possibly turn his host into an alcoholic.

An intellectual who sends too much energy to his brain-genius, will be in danger of imbalance in varying forms.

We can therefore see that in the human being we have an extensive double network (head and body) of individual activities, all needing to be mastered, co-ordinated and oriented by a master-will, the lord of the whole entity.

And who is that lord?

That is the 'I' to which we have referred, the real 'will' and the real identity behind it all. This identity is the essential *you,* the source of your present existence in your present form. It is the only force strong enough to control and to make a success of all the warring and perhaps greedy elements of your personality, run by its set of endocrine glands and all that they represent.

Continuing our search regarding the glands and their activities we come finally to the greatest mystery in all this mysterious subject. The strange little living form which composes the human brain is found to be hermaphrodite, male and female in one. As a true hermaphrodite, it is able to give birth to a new being. But in this case, the new being will be a spiritual entity or instrument, capable of awareness and activity in the invisible world of causes.

This entity which can be brought to birth in the brain of man has been known by many names. In ancient civilisations, such as the Egyptian, it was represented by one or more serpents rearing up from the brow, the serpent being the symbol of super-wisdom. In India, a knob on the forehead represented the awakened 'Third Eye'. In China, the mandarins (sages) were allowed to wear the peacock's feather on their head-dress, also representing the Eye of Initiation.

We are therefore considering a phenomenon which has always held first place of importance in ancient knowledge. The explanation of the mystery is that earnest aspiration and one-pointed application in a human being raise his rate of vibration, producing new stimulations which produce changes and developments in the glands. Eventually, and especially, the Pineal and the Pituitary are aroused to a new livingness. They are stimulated to the point when new vibrations and new radiations are set up. These finally impinge upon each other. Then the wonderful 'marriage' within the head, between the Pituitary (representing the female and physical aspects) and the Pineal (representing the male and spiritual aspects) takes place. When this happens, the *real* consciousness, the 'Christ

Child' is *born,* and the sacred Third Eye glows into being.

Christ said 'When thine eye be single thy whole body shall be full of light'—which is a very good description of the whole situation. By this new light all mysteries and all knowledge is eventually illumined; and 'all that is hidden shall be made plain'.

The 'Christ Child' is no vague phenomenon. It is the *essential* spiritual man, a being of power and creativity in the world of causes, the world of actual reality. From then onwards, man becomes a walking spirit, serving the Plan of Creation with growing awareness. Such a glorious future is the outcome of one-pointed devotion to a life of service for humanity and for all the kingdoms in nature.

To be fundamentally a free awakened spirit, bathed in the glory of God-consciousness—such is the hidden goal awaiting those who persevere! For the average man it is a long, long road, and results will come about naturally in the far dim future. But for those who 'take the Kingdom of Heaven by violence' through sacrifice, prayer, fasting and meditation, the way is much shortened, and anything becomes possible.

Such achievement is the birthright of the real *you,* that essential 'I'—that spark of the soul embedded in matter which is yourself. When God said 'I will make man in my image' what did He mean? It is, of course, only possible for us to postulate or visualise God in a tiny degree. The Teaching, however, is that God divided Himself into Male (Spirit) and Female (Matter) so that when these two fused the result of such a marriage was Consciousness, the Son Christ. That which can take place within the head of man is certainly a minute 'image' of that activity of the Creator.

Man's ultimate achievement is to bear a spirit-son within his Hermaphrodite brain, and thus join the ranks of the spirit-world whilst still in bodily form. This is the glory, the power, the love and the Light which has been known and glimpsed throughout history. It is inexpressible in words because it by-passes the intellect. Many attempts have been made to describe the ineffable achievement of spiritual consciousness. The

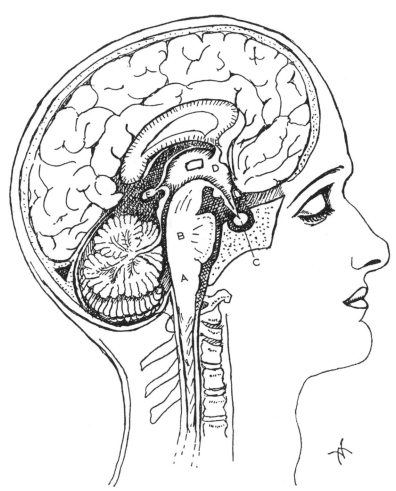

As the result of a dedicated life, transmuted energies rise up the spinal nerve channel, into the Medulla Oblongata, (A) through the Pons or Mid-Brain, (B) then pass down into the Pituitary Gland (C) (behind the eyes). The increasing Pituitary radiations finally pass through the Third Ventricle (D) (or air cavity) until they awaken the dormant Pineal, (E) and the Third Eye lights up between them.

(Drawn by the author from specimens in the Royal College of Surgeons, London)

Buddha called it simply 'Nirvana'. But in these days of the urgently enquiring mind, the need for realisation is acute. Such a one as Krishnamurti has spent many devoted years trying to teach men the way to the 'Nirvana' which he has reached. But the inner world can only be an individual experience, recognised in another without words.

Such an experience gives freedom through discipline, power through humility, riches through deprivation, achievement through selfless service. It comes after turning all our worldly ideas inside out. It is the prerogative and heritage of the essential 'I' within each one of us.

Therefore, in our first approach to the challenging adventure which lies before us, we should go straight to the fountain head, the real 'I'. We must *become* that 'I', so to speak, instead of being at the mercy of all the conflicting acquisitive glandular powers developing within our personal kingdom.

But what, actually, is the 'I'? What is its nature, its needs, its activities?

Is it not best summed up in three words—love, beauty and achievement—words which can interact to mean the same thing—*fulfilment*?—and is not that kind of fulfilment what the real 'I' lives for? Search yourself in this.

However, if we want to describe what exactly love, beauty and fulfilment are, we are up against the impossible. For they represent the mystery of reality, the mystery of being and of realisation. We can only say that love and beauty and achievement are demonstrations and qualities which we can only experience through our endocrine glandular system when it is health. For these glands lie behind and cause to function all our organs. Therefore the reactions of sight, hearing, feeling, all of the five senses, depend on our glandular perfection; whilst the realisations of abstract thought, of those appreciations which allow the entry of love, awe, wonder and worship, depend on the centres within head and heart.

Therefore a serious student of Meditation seeks to build up his glands into as perfect a state as possible, so that they can become good recipients of the forces and intelligencies which play through the ether nuclei behind them.

How, though, can we build an equalised and perfected glandular system? The ingredients needed are, firstly, right motive, together with correct posture, controlled breathing, correct nourishment, and forgetting the self in service, and Meditation.

For, when once we recognise the existence of our glands and the part they have to play, it is better to forget them, and focus on the over-all aim, that of love—service—fulfilment. The saying is: 'Energy follows thought'. This is important to remember. Whatever we think about draws energy to itself like a magnet—or we could say that the mind projects energy to the object of its thought. So we could easily over-stimulate one of our glands by giving it undue attention.

On the other hand, it would be difficult to give too much attention to our ideals, our wish for integrity, and our purpose in life—for we wish to attract all the energies within our being to the one focal point of the desired achievement. When we do this, the glands will safely adjust themselves and balance up in their development.

We now come to a more mysterious part of our technique. We have to bring our imagination into play and visualise those activities within ourselves which cannot be seen. It is necessary to realise that there is a difference between the functions of the visible physical body, the invisible electrical counterpart, the living emotional reactions, the varied mental activities, and the subtle abstract realisations and ideals. All these are separate, living entities, as it were, each one trying to usurp power over the whole! A person can be a slave to any of his physical appetites. He can be galvanised into extreme activity either under emotional or mental or spiritual stimulus. The uncontrolled emotional stimulation is exhausting; the mental stimulation is equally so. But the stimulation which comes from the soul has a calming effect and feeds the nervous system with the 'peace which passeth understanding'—because, in fact, the understanding has been by-passed!

The soul lives in a world of its own, the stratum of soul-vibrations. It has a task to perform. It must become the intermediary between the world of spirit (a world of still higher vibration) and the physical or brain world. It performs this function by acting, because of its pellucid calmness, as a mirror which can reflect spiritual truth (or the Universal Mind) down into matter (or the physical mind and brain). But in this case, matter, in the form of the vibrations of brain, emotions and intellect, has also to become pellucid, calm and mirror-like, in order to receive the reflection of spiritual truth via the soul.

The above gives you the simple problem which faces the aspirant to Meditation. He has to learn to produce stillness in his body, emotions and mind, so that together they constitute one calm chalice which can receive and reflect truth as a quiet pool can perfectly reflect the sun. In such quietness also the auditory nerve can distinguish the 'still small voice' of real consciousness. So that some may learn from the soul world visually, some through hearing, and again some through the intuition, which needs neither sight nor sound nor form—it simply KNOWS. But first of all, the student is trying to build himself into a sort of television for the reception of spiritual truth and wisdom. He is also trying to gain control so that he can, in his Meditation, plug in to different stations in the invisible worlds. His success will depend upon the quality of his motive and his visualisation. For each type of thought or feeling has its own wavelength which through resonance will attract its corresponding higher octaves, as it were.

A person cannot suddenly determine to have high motives and pure aspiration. These qualities must be built into the framework of his personality until they become its essential expression. Such development is obtained through the different stages of Meditation. In fact it can well be stated that Meditation is something which *happens* when finally the aspirant has, through selfless service, one-pointed study and patient exercise and training, produced the right conditions.

When young people dash out to a Maharishi in India for

training in the achievement of revelation, they do so because instinctively they know what they desire. But when they return and, with splendid sensibility, get to work to serve the old and the poor, they have chosen the best way to achieve their fulfilment. Somehow or other they have made the discovery, so difficult for us all, that self-interest is the great imprisoner; that egotism or self-centredness creates a shell around us which is the strongest form of isolationism in existence. For it cuts off the life-flow between all living creatures. It short-circuits and inhibits our realisation and our creative expression. It can eventually produce mental atrophy and render us abnormal.

Therefore the main enemy we have to conquer is selfishness; the main friend we have to make is our own highest aspiration. Thus prepared, we can now take up the study of the systems of development which are necessarily associated with the practice of Meditation so that we will have a glimpse of the pattern of achievement that leads to the glorious heritage of man.

2

First Steps in Meditation

As we survey the dim vistas in the history of Meditation, we must ask ourselves which we will select for our initial exploration.

Shall we delve into the extensive knowledge of the Yogis? Shall we consider the extremist measures of the Zen Buddhists? or the rather cold austerities of the Western monks? And what about the Temple Mysteries of Egypt and Greece?

What did Christ teach His Disciples in regard to Meditation? How far has the Christian Church developed or understood it?

What do such groups as the Theosophists or the Rosicrucians recommend, from their approach outside of orthodoxy?

On surveying all this panorama of choice, it would seem sensible to select the method which has stood the test of time, and has been most nearly used by one and all.

Therefore we will outline the classic pattern which has come down to us throughout the ages, and is still recommended today. And we will call it 'Classic Meditation'. It has been and is in use, either partly or completely, by many cultures. But it is better to judge a system on its own merits than by its exact ancestry.

Classic Meditation, then, is divided into four stages. These are: Concentration, Meditation, Contemplation and Adoration.

These four stages constitute the whole act of Meditation,

and they exist as the Crown and centre of the life of a disciple on the Path of the good life. This Crown exists in its own setting, which includes, as we have said, the practice of harm- lessness, love, humane diet, scientific breathing, bodily culture, selfless service, and the study of spiritual laws.

All this has been touched upon fairly clearly in our other books, and we know the rudiments of humane good health, as well as the vistas of inner and outer achievement which lie ahead. And we know that our first task will be to gain mastery over those habits of thought which still hold us back.

For our aid, therefore, it is recommended that we practise, without fail, three simple exercises, as well as our Meditation. These are known as the morning resolve, the evening review, and the spiritual diary. The morning resolve is entered into just after awakening. It is the act of tuning in to the day's programme from the highest attitude we can manage, deter- mining to be what we truly wish to be in face of whatever unpleasant or tempting moments the day may bring. We must do this confidently and joyfully, with no question of failure, but conscious of the spiritual help we will earnestly need.

The evening review takes place before we fall asleep at night. We carefully go over the events of the day, and see how far we have measured up to difficulties and opportunities and new experiences. We do this quite impartially, not blaming or praising ourselves at all—but just *looking,* and admitting the facts we discover. Krishnamurti has said that when we become able correctly to do this, we will remould our characters. By doing this review we also help to melt away our subconscious inhibitions, regrets and fears. In fact we go through an atom of 'Purgatory' day by day, dissolving its elements, so that in the end, it is said, there will be no 'Purgatory' awaiting us in the future, and we will find ourselves free, compared to what we otherwise would have been.

The spiritual diary is kept day by day after Meditation. In it we note everything to do with new realisations, new aspira- tions, new ideas or ideals, which come to us either during the Meditation or during the twenty-four hours. In this way we can keep track of what is actually happening to our development, our sense of values, and our touch with the spiritual world. It is also a necessary training in self expression.

All this may sound rather a formidable programme. But remember that even in learning to ride a bicycle we start with nervousness and difficulty and many complications, although in the end it all becomes simple and automatic. Classic Meditation is not a complicated process so long as one knows what one is trying to do. Once understood, it will fall into place as the natural way of living a real and progressive life. Certainly it is not nearly such a trial as learning a language, mathematics or even the piano. All that is needed is the strength of mind to put first things first—in which case the short daily intervals dedicated to Meditation should take priority over breakfast, dinner and tea, over gossip—television—even over superfluous hours of sleep! For we are seeking the richest of all prizes.

We begin, therefore, by deciding which part of the day we can best reserve for our initial self-training, and in which sequestered place we will work. Usually the privacy of our bedroom is the best choice. If, however, we are denied this especial privacy then we must find a corner in house, garden or park, a museum, a river bank—some place where we can pass daily a period alone without attracting attention. In such a place we will be building an invisible sanctuary which will retain the vibrations of our aspiration so that it becomes increasingly easy for us to tune in.

Of course the ideal place is our own bed, or the floor of our bedroom, so let us consider this as possible. We can prepare by removing any oppressive clothing or shoes, and, naturally, bathing hands and face in cool water to remove our contact with the outer world. We then settle ourselves in the position which seems most suitable for us. The ancient Egyptian Pharaohs meditated whilst seated on a straight chair or throne, with a hand on either knee. There are many statues of them in this pose in the world's museums. The Indian Buddhas prefer to sit cross-legged on the ground. In their 'Lotus' position, the soles of the feet are turned upwards, and the body so locked into place that it would be impossible to fall over should they pass into a trance. The hands are in various positions according to the kind of meditation in progress.

But the beginner has only to remember a few things. Firstly, it is important to keep the spine upright, so that the back is not hollow, and the chin is not sticking out. If the spine is straight and balanced upon itself, the spiritual channel will be unimpeded, and the nerves and sinews can remain at rest.

As soon as the body is quite comfortable and at peace, we turn our attention to our breathing. Here again, we are at the door of an extensive science. But at first all we must think about is to reduce our breathing to a slow, quiet rhythm, without strain, inducing peace and relaxation, and under our control.

We next take a look at our emotional state. We must be careful not intensely to desire or anticipate anything at all. We are offering ourselves for whatever our Creator prefers for us, and we cannot know what that may be. If we have brought ourselves to accept that all that happens is for the best, we have taken a big step. Our only task will be to understand!

Having quietened our emotions, we pass on to the mind. Here, indeed, we have to be stern. For the mind is the greatest tyrant whom we have to face. It is *determined* that we shall not by-pass it into the realms of wisdom and enlightenment. For then it would lose its power over us. So it fights us, with doubts, with fatigue, with endless interrupting thoughts, with illusions, with 'wishful thinking', with ambition, with excuses! Oh, well was it said by the ancients: 'The mind is the enemy of the real!' Evidently they knew— but evidently, also, they conquered, else they could never have made that saying.

One of the things which keeps up an endless disturbance in the mind is a guilty conscience, either when it is raging in the front of the mind or buried and repressed in the background.

In Meditation we are offering ourselves utterly to the spiritual or higher world. We are laying the gift of ourselves on the altar of our aspiration. It must be a clean and clear offering. Christ told us to delay our offering at the altar if we had any quarrel with our brother man; to go and make peace with him first, so that there was nothing on our conscience.

This is very important. You would not expect your watch or your car to function if there was sediment or grit in the works. The mind also, if it is to function properly, must be free from the sediment of old repressed thoughts and resentments. These create a shell through which light cannot penetrate. The evening review is invaluable for curing this situation. We should realise that if anyone has offended us, that represents a test of our acceptance, understanding, sense of values, sense of humour—in fact, common sense! The offence is, actually, of no importance whatsoever except as a little five-finger exercise in character-building—*our* character, not the offender's! So we wipe out any such trivialities from our minds, and enlarge our focus towards the mind of God!

Having wrestled gently but firmly until we have reduced our mind to calm co-operation, we are at last ready for the first stage of the Meditational process—that of *Concentration*. This consists in bringing the whole of our personality to a one-pointed consideration of a selected subject or object. If this is correctly done, our physical brain, emotional radiations, mental capacities—*all* having been reduced to a condition of quietness and calmness, fuse together into one amalgamated pool of intention and attention. This is a 'pool' so still that it becomes a reflector of whatever part of truth we shall touch or tune in to.

This complete attention of all our being is what we know as Concentration. It often happens involuntarily, as when we are reading so thrilling a book that we do not notice the greatest disturbance around us. But to do it deliberately is another matter.

As soon as we have achieved that state of Concentration as far as we are able, we pass into the second stage, that of Meditation itself. For this we have to choose our subject or object. As it is a thought which will give birth to others, it is sometimes known as the 'seed-thought'. The beginner had better choose as simple an object as possible, such as a flower, a tool, an ornament, something which he has often noticed.

We then begin to visualise this object, building it up clearly in our mind's eye, until we could almost draw and paint it. As soon as this visualisation is as complete as we can make it, we next begin to *think* about the object, summing up all we know about its origins, its use, its quality and its future. Whilst we are doing this we will be astonished at the realisations and appreciations which we are able to feel, not hitherto experienced. We know more about the object than we thought we did. When we reach the zenith of our Meditation we could write quite an interesting essay about this object, so comparatively casually noticed until now, for we have reached the stage of 'Creative Meditation'.

It is at this point that we have to become very careful. We must hold all that we have so far achieved steadily at attention whilst we pass on to the third stage—that of *Contemplation*. We have built a 'thought-form' of our object. This is not something vague and misty. It is an actual potent creation in the ether, or mind-world. It is a form which now has its own vibration and wavelength, which align it with all similar vibrations flowing through the entire universe. You have created a little radio-station. Supposing that you have built a rose! Because of its resonance with the whole rose world, your thought-form is plugged in to it. However, at present your thought-form is full of your own limited thoughts and conceptions.

But if you were able quietly to withdraw those thoughts, leaving the form empty, and wait, you would see a change. Your ether-rose will become a vacuum which will draw into it all life of similar vibration. Therefore if you stop all your own thinking and watch attentively, *new* (to you) knowledge will flow through the rose to you, new information as to the meaning purpose, beauties and potentialities of the world of roses. In fact, according to your ability, you are drawing upon the Universal Mind, the Mind of God.

This is what we call 'inspiration'. We are inspiring or

inhaling knowledge or wisdom. Having done our part, and worked to attain the state of Contemplation—life takes over and teaches *us,* and we must take care only to listen and attend, not to think. This is what is sometimes called 'making one's mind a blank', but you will realise that it is nothing of the sort. We have attempted, however imperfectly, to build within our brain a channel to the Universal Mind where all is known. This channel, if we persist in all the pattern of training so far indicated, will grow stronger and stronger until it is as real and as useful as anything within us. This channel is a bridge between the inner world of causes and of knowledge to the little organs in our brain which can learn to interpret and step down that which comes through to us.

This bridge was known in the ancient Eastern training as the Antahkarana. It is often referred to in mystic literature. It is also sometimes called 'The Rainbow Bridge'—a beautiful name, and for a beautiful reason. When it is perfected it will be formed of seven strands, looking like Neon lighting, of the seven colours of the rainbow. These seven strands represent in miniature the seven qualities upon which our solar system is formed, each having its own colour, function, character and sound.

The mysteries of Meditation include many other fascinating discoveries. For instance, what is the contribution of the individual spark of spirit which we know as the 'I'? The 'I' represents the real inner *Will,* a tiny fraction of the Will of God. The 'I' determines the focus of the whole person.

If the focus is on the highest good and the highest achievement possible, the whole tone and vibration of the person is gradually raised—that is to say that all the atoms in body, emotions and mind are stepped up to ever higher rates of vibration. This is the process of transmutation. Eventually the glands and centres all up the spine are transmuted to the extent that the whole spine contains a living circulating stream of power entirely interacting. The aspiration of prayer and meditation which is instigated in the centres in the head acts as a magnet to the forces in the spinal channel, drawing them upwards. They arrive at the top of the spine, where is the medulla oblongata. The Rainbow Bridge is being built near this junction. Here the union of spirit and matter takes place, as we have already noted. The forces coming up the spinal channel from the spinal centres stimulate the Pituitary body into increased action and vibration; whilst the spiritual forces drawn down through the Rainbow Bridge from the highest centre above the head (known as the Thousand Petalled Lotus) stimulate the Pineal (male spiritual) gland into action. When this takes place, the 'marriage' is achieved between spirit and matter, and the 'Son' (spiritual consciousness—the Christ Child) emerges into being, in the form of the THIRD EYE.

Much has been written about the fires which lie dormant in the lower spinal centres, fires and forces known by the ancient name of the 'Kundalini'. In a developing human being these eventually rise up the spine from centre to centre, finally reaching the domain of the Pituitary body and the Pineal gland.

The Kundalini expresses real electric fire, although subtle. This fire burns away any dross or impurity in its path. If there is much impurity (dregs of an egoistic mind or of an impure life) the conflagration produced is so great that it may injure or destroy the brain. This would result in the many unexplained cases of obsession, split personality, insanity or paralysis, the more puzzling because they often have occurred in people of very advanced although unequal development.

It is therefore essential carefully to purify the way of life if one intends to speed up the inner development. That is why esoteric training has been kept partly secret and given out with circumspection and supervision. An advanced Teacher or Guru is able clairvoyantly to see the condition of his pupil's centres and the degree of purity attained within his personality, and thereby gauge the training for which he is ready. If his integrity and his surrender is complete the time will come for the Kundalini fires to rise safely, stimulating the action between Pineal and Pituitary, so that the THIRD EYE successfully opens, and the wonderful access to the spiritual world takes place.

This glorious admittance consciously into the 'presence of God' becomes a permanent state of being. It gives health, power and initiative, because the recipient has prepared himself to receive and to keep it. If, however, a person in ignorance of these facts proceeds to seek for artificial stimulation of his powers and bring on a forcing process through unwise breathing exercises, unsuitable yogic practices, or the use of drugs such as L.S.D., he will most certainly bring about new experiences, good or bad, dangerous or abortive.

But, obviously, if the character, the way of living and the understanding have not been devotedly developed, the recipient of these experiences will either be in danger of permanent brain damage, or disorientation of moral set-up; and in any case he or she will not know how to interpret or what to do about any impressions received. Although there may be great exaltation and thrills at the time, it surely does not need L.S.D. to convince an observant person that the inner creative world exists and is bound to be marvellous! But it is also bound to be so full, and complicated, that only a character based on integrity could find its way, through *resonance,* to the sphere desired.

When, however, the Rainbow Bridge has been well built, through service, meditation, and surrender of the self, the experiences which come are coherent, constructive and productive of inspired action. The recipient goes hopefully and steadily forward because he has become aware of the goal.

In a fully developed and rounded-out character, each strand of the Rainbow Bridge is growing fairly equally, so that in Meditation the student obtains a balanced, although preliminary, channel to the inner worlds. This is why it is important to learn to live the 'whole life', even if little by little, and not to think that any part of it can be left until 'later on'. In that way, imbalance could obtain, and spoil achievement.

What do we mean by the 'whole life'? We have written about this in our other books. But, *very* briefly, when man begins really to mature, he asks himself what he *is*, and what he is here for? A little study will show him that he is the only thinking and creative medium between the Creator and this planet, with its contents of all the kingdoms of nature. Man has it in his power to devastate this planet with soil erosion, and with various other pollutions—or to nurse it towards its highest potential of beauty and fertility. He has it in his power to destroy the soil, water, plant and animal worlds, as well as his own species—or he can learn, through Meditation, the Plan of Evolution, and take on his true responsibility as Guardian, under God, of all that lives and is at his mercy.

This spirit of Guardianship comes alive in a mature person. He then has a great need to know how best to use it. Our books aspire to answer this need. The awakened person considers always what are the results of his acts and his needs. He watches the effects of his way of life on himself and all that he contains; on the animal and plant kingdoms; and on world economy. He realises that no good ever comes out of violence, out of exploitation, self-indulgence or compromise.

Eventually he faces up to his relationship with the animal kingdom. Finally he becomes what we know as a humanitarian. He recognises that to live by Love is the only way in which to produce a sane and bountiful world. From then on he begins to live the 'whole life' in measure as he understands it, and as well as he can. He refuses to devour his younger brothers, the animals, knowing himself to be, as science acknowledges, of the fruitarian species; he refuses to slay his brother man in warfare, or to destroy his own body and brain through wrong living.

He recognises the outer world as God's Garment, and the care of it as his Holy responsibility. He seeks out his comrades in spirit, people who already feel as he does. Together they work for the welfare of animals, trees, plants, soil and water. These people are the hope—the only hope—for the coming of a New Age.

A student at this stage realises that man's function is to combine three entities—firstly he must become the perfect animal, and consciously a fruitarian species. Secondly, he must become the perfect human being, whose creative mind can mediate between all the kingdoms of nature. Thirdly, he must align with his spiritual soul, who is already an inhabitant of the Heaven world. All these three combine in man to give him his unique place on earth. When he lives according to these realisations, he begins to demonstrate the 'whole life'. He cannot by-pass his obligations in any sphere. He knows that a life of sharing must replace that of exploitation; that to love one's neighbour as oneself includes also one's neighbour animal and plant.

This of course will produce a quite new way of life. It necessitates the breakdown of all self-protection and self-interest. For the new man must hold out his hand to the younger generation, give what he can of the light coming to him, and stand up honestly for his new morality. He finds that he is no longer alone, but that thousands of fellow-spirits the world over are moving into the new way of the 'whole life'. From then on he need never be lonely again, or uninspired or unoccupied. His life expands in value, in meaning, in inspiration and in joy.

True, he can see and feel the vast sea of suffering and of evil which exists everywhere. But he learns that one only grows through suffering and through finding out how to cure its origins.

Life has become a challenge! The new man or woman wants desperately to achieve as healthy a body and brain as possible IN ORDER TO SERVE. If it has been possible to develop the greatest quality of all—that of Integrity—then only the 'whole life' will suffice in future.

3

Inspiration in the Highlands

We have outlined the first three stages in the process of Meditation, as well as the development of character and of realisation which its practice will bring. It may take considerable time before the fourth and final stage, which we know as Adoration, is achieved. Nevertheless, eventually there comes a time when, having been shown, in Contemplation, the wonders of God's design, whether in a butterfly's wing, an atom of mineral, or a solar system, or the mystery of a human character, something happens. The student is suddenly overwhelmed by wonder, and by a new realisation of the utter loving magnificence of what has been designed. His appreciation is so deep that he becomes *identified,* as it were, with the fraction of the Creator's mind which he has been allowed to touch, and he passes into the state of Adoration.

This last stage is impossible, of course, to describe. It has been known as ecstasy, bliss, Nirvana, and it exists in various degrees. But it comes best to those who not only love the Creator but strive to develop their understanding of His Plan of Evolution, in order that they may serve it.

We have given a picture of one of the more simple, well-tried and age-old methods of Meditation, as it has been brought down to us. But to feel attracted to it one must have graduated out from the purely emotional focus of the mystic who only wants to *feel,* and be ready to train and discipline the mind in order to *know.* If we are not ready for that, the above description will make us recoil at the thought of so much apparent complication.

We may also ask ourselves, what, after all, is the difference between Meditation and prayer? Prayer is usually a request for favours and for forgiveness. Meditation is an effort to learn and to co-operate with the Divine Will. It is the contribution of a mind which is reaching maturity.

Both prayer and Meditation have their rightful places, expressed for us thus :

'Ask and it shall be given unto you.' (prayer)

'Seek and ye shall find.' (Meditation)

A child asks. An adult finds.

Of course only a certain percentage of seekers feel drawn to the rhythm of training described above. It may even be that one is an atheist, not believing in anything, yet still trying to seek 'logically' for the meaning and purpose of life. Such a one, all unknowingly, might outclass his more pious brethren in honesty, kindness and determination. A person who scoffs at the theory of Meditation might yet be training himself for it very effectively, as a bridge-player, or a designer of computers! We must reserve judgment of all that we see. We must seek only to *see* it, impartially, and always to seek.

Impartiality will safeguard us from many mistakes.

The strands of the Rainbow Bridge are the channels which link us, first of all, with the Planetary Consciousness. At this preliminary stage we recognise that this earth is the living body of a great conscious Entity, in whom we live, move and have our being, and with whom we can eventually co-operate.

After much further development we will recognise that our solar system itself is the living body of a greater conscious Entity, with Whom we are intimately connected. We have then passed from Planetary Consciousness into Solar Consciousness. In the dim future we can look forward to the time when we will have built our Rainbow Bridge of such material that we become linked up with the Cosmos outside the solar system; and we recognise a still more awesome Life. We are then beginning to touch what is known as 'Cosmic Consciousness', in small or greater degree.

The term 'Cosmic Consciousness' has been bandied about and often wrongly used to designate lesser types of consciousness. As we know, there is much wishful thinking and claim-making in the world today, by people whose understanding of what is Holy and sacred and unutterable falls far short of the desirable. In their amateur eagerness, many 'rush in where Angels fear to tread'. Those who, through their own humility and patient efforts, have been privileged to have unity with the higher consciousness and the higher wisdom, never speak about it. That is the golden rule.

Such people can only be recognised through one's own growing intuition. They keep quiet, very quiet. But by their thought and Meditation they will be doing much to save this world from the insanity in which it is dangerously wallowing at this time.

We can see, therefore, that the science of Meditation is the beginning of a long and glorious trail, known as the 'Path', or the 'Way', or the 'Light'. Those of us who make a start can take it very gradually and simply. But the motive and perseverance *must* be there, and also the sort of understanding which we have outlined in these chapters, of what it is all about.

If we wish to enlarge our studies, we will have a fascinating search, whether we explore the knowledge of the Japanese Samurai, the Chinese Buddhists, or the Zen Buddhists themselves. We have mentioned the Oracles of Ancient Egypt. These were usually women, kept in the Temples and dedicated to a type of Meditation which enabled them to make bold pronouncements and to prophesy. From time immemorial the greatest of all men was the Prophet. He was one who had touched the inner worlds and brought back glimpses of the future through Meditation. His help was the factor of most value to any ancient nation. The long centuries of Egyptian culture spread their influence far and wide. The same understanding of Divine Laws can be traced in most of the succeeding civilisations. Some writers believe[1] that it was only when mankind took to a life of carnivorism, warfare and materialism, that this great fundamental culture became obscured and forgotten. Then humanity passed into the Dark Ages, whilst superstition and bigotry flourished.

At the present period in history 'materialism has hanged itself', so to speak, and fully shown what it is worth and in what it results. All the wise ones, therefore, are now turning their backs on materialism and seeking once more the ways of truth, integrity, joy and freedom. God is answering their quest by bringing to their notice the fundamental way of Revelation through Meditation.

Having given this bare outline about what classic Meditation is and what it can do, our next step will be to show, from an actual example, how it works out. The finest Meditation which I ever experienced resulted in this book, *The Fifth Dimension*.

It happened in this way.

In 1938 I was living in London, and deeply engrossed in writing my second book, *The Initiation of the World*. My family asked me to go away with them for a really restful holiday in Scotland, and to take no work or books with me at all. To this I agreed. So, one day, I found myself utterly alone in a wild Scottish Highland near our friend's tiny Manse, our whole party having gone for a tour.

The weather was warm and gracious. The contrast between the life and work of London, and this silent loneliness was startling. I sat on the grass, and could see nothing all around me but the line of the horizon and the clear sky.

'What a chance,' I thought, 'for a real Meditation! I will see how far I can get with it. And I will choose a subject about which I know *nothing*! I have never read Einstein's work. I will Meditate upon the Fourth Dimension and see if I can discover it for myself. I will then seek to formulate a Fifth Dimension. I will then Contemplate on the results which such types of knowledge could and will bring to humanity!'

[1] See *The Recovery of Culture* by Henry Bailey Stevens (Daniel & Co.).

Having thus set myself what I thought was a quite impossible task, but one which presented a real test of the value of this ancient science, I settled down with a feeling of timelessness and peaceful opportunity. After some time I realised that my Meditation was developing happily along all its stages, and that I seemed to be making my own assessments and discoveries.

I recounted this Meditation exactly as it came to me, in my third book, *The Fifth Dimension,* written down in 1940. Today, 1969, I am only slightly modifying it to align it with present events. The future which is foreseen is that of the next century and onwards. The exciting history of events and discoveries which has followed on since 1939 are discussed in my other books.

If it is thought that some of the ensuing chapters lie in the realm of 'wishful thinking', let us bear in mind that every reform, achievement and discovery *must* be preceded by a 'wish' and then 'thinking' or making thought-forms (which are actually the powerful foundations of all that happens on this planet).

Surely when humanity reaches maturity it will run the world collectively and coherently in this way. All who begin now to use with integrity the powers of the mind will be helping to give this chaotic world what it most needs—a collective *mind,* activated by goodwill and enthusiasm. They will be helping themselves to reach spiritual adulthood and human efficiency, and become a power for good and for constructive co-operation.

The following outline of our experiment falls quite naturally into phases just described. At first we will 'set the stage', as it were; studying the environment of the problem we intend to solve, our chosen 'seed-thought'. Thus the first stage of Concentration is built up. We then pass into actual Meditation, considering all sides and potentialities of our subject and seeing how much we can arrive at through the contents and exercise of our own mind, in both its concrete and abstract aspects. We may be surprised, even at this stage, at the conclusions to which we will come, without the aid of any books, other than those already within our memory.

After assembling all that we possibly can of buddings and rootlets which spring from our seed-thought, we pass into the third stage, that of Contemplation. This is where we wait for miracles to happen, streams of new realisations and prognostications to arrive, as precious gifts from the Universal Mind. This is where we can perhaps register a new 'discovery' to add to the riches of human evolution.

One last important word. Let us not neglect prayer. Prayer is perhaps more necessary than Meditation, and should be put first, in the way that walking comes before running. The preceding chapters seek merely to show that Meditation, and in fact all growth in constructive thinking and mental development, is a scientific and factual activity. It is not vague and its success depends fundamentally upon the purity of motive and the wholeheartedness of purpose which is the foundation of our being.

Therefore, once these chapters have been digested, as it were, it is better not to become intellectually engrossed with the subject of mental development, but to put first things first; to cleanse and to strengthen one's life-motive, one's power of loving all creation and one's readiness to help and serve without reservations. In the latter case, our inner development will take place in the safest and best way, under soul care. As regards Meditation, having once understood the necessity for the successive stages described, one eventually goes through them *habitually* as a natural and essential process. One realises that anyone who makes a success of any concentrated endeavour must have been, in his own way, in Meditation. The only difference is that in the case of this book we seek to work for spiritual rather than material inspiration.

PART II
From Concentration to Meditation

4

Statement of Our Problem

(FIRST STAGE)

It is clear that so far human beings are not managing their world very well. There is something wrong somewhere. It seems difficult to find anyone to blame but themselves. They have been placed upon a planet which continues to roll unerringly upon its appointed path. The seasons follow each other with faithful regularity. Upon this revolving home they can find everything calculated to give them their hearts' desires. Infinite beauties and infinite delights are theirs for the taking. There are just enough difficulties and varieties to keep them stimulated. There is sufficient space, sufficient nourishment and sufficient occupation for all.

In themselves, human beings have been given amazing bodies, whose natural state is that of joyful health and energy. They have been given mental powers whose possibilities are immeasurable, and creative ability which is allowing them to master all the substances and forces of nature one by one. They have been provided throughout their history with a succession of leaders and teachers who have bequeathed to them doctrines and laws which, although quite simple, would ensure an ideal social life.

What have they succeeded in making out of this wonderfully generous heritage of theirs? Has generosity begot generosity in their hearts, or beauty aroused thankfulness? Has strength flowered to further strength, and opportunity led to wisdom? The picture before us of human quality and human achievement is kaleidoscopic, showing closely intermingling facets of beauty, of worth, of genius, of bestiality, of idiocy and of crime. It is difficult indeed to pronounce judgment upon this jangled pattern, to discern whether its greatest trend is towards the light or towards the darkness. Man has made of his world a patchwork of disconnected bits and pieces. His most obvious lack seems to be that of *coherency.*

Within his world of plenty he has produced want. In face of the ordered march of nature he often produces disorder, disharmony, discord, disconnectedness. Capable of creating beauty, he yet seems content to dwell mostly in conditions of hopeless ugliness. Of his magnificent body he makes on the whole a travesty. His mind, as an actual potent instrument, he usually ignores altogether. He sets self-preservation as his goal, yet bends all his efforts and his wits to the production of conditions which result in wars, disease, and other methods of self-destruction. His mental life must habituate itself to a code of contradictions, misfits, conflictions and inadequacies which inhibit coherent thought.

In many ways the present life of humanity presents a quite mad spectacle to the unbiased eye.

Yet withal, the average human being desires supremely to live happily and safely, to enjoy beauty and comfort and good-fellowship, and the stimulation of achievement.

Where, then, is the missing link between man and his desires? What is the hidden error which dislocates his life?

IT MUST BE FOUND. Until it is discovered and recognised humanity will continue to wallow in the quagmire of confusion and destruction into which it has plunged. When powerful nations treat other nations, without apology, to anarchy, robbery, slaughter and persecution and the only remedy which can be found is further slaughter by those who would keep the peace (!), it is indeed no longer a world in which anyone can shirk the urgent responsibility for putting things straight, and for establishing a new and a better order.

For it must be the past apathy and unconcern of every man which has brought the world to the terrible impasse that obtains today. The leaders of men can only act as public opinion or public strength of mind or character allow them. Dictators can, and do in part, mould public opinion, but alternatively they can be moulded by it. Most strong men are both potential tyrants and potential benefactors. The issue is largely determined by the desires of the people around them— their 'environment'. Only a definite social condition allows a certain type of leader to come to power. It is the mentality of the public—made up of the mentalities of yourself and of my-self—which rules the issue. The responsibility lies largely at our door.

If this is so, then there is but one remedy for present world chaos. It is for each one of us to begin at once to do our share of thinking, and help to make public opinion an entirely new and courageous and clear and omnipotent thing. Then, and only then, can we deserve and expect a new and splendid world in which to live—a splendid world which is there all the time, but from which we shut ourselves out simply by lack of thought.

I suppose each of us believes that we *do* think. Yet I fear that almost all of us are quite incapable of real thinking. Our first step should be to realise this dangerous defection and start to remedy it.

In order properly to estimate our habitual lack of thought the best procedure is—to think! In these chapters we are going to carry through a train of clear, logical and original thinking (we hope!) proving first of all what a thrilling adventure that is, and secondly what miracles of quite new knowledge it will bring to us. Wise men have always declared that there is nothing the human mind cannot learn, without books, purely through a system of scientifically controlling the mind. This art is practised either consciously, subconsciously, or in part by anyone who produces an original idea or creation.

Let us consider what we mean when we talk about thinking. The average person does not think at all. His brain, under various stimuli from his environment, reacts almost automatic-ally. It produces ideas and phrases for him. These it either picks up like a wireless receiver from the crowded ether, or repeats from its own stored memory. It is almost impossible for the average person to pronounce a sentence or an idea or state a fact which is not merely lifted from his memory, either from what he has read, learnt, or heard. Most people do not realise that this is so.

Thinking, however, is a function entirely different from this repetitive process. It is an act of creation. It produces something which was not there before, at any rate in the mind of the thinker. It puts two and two together. It compares, sifts, analyses, deducts, questions, and results in a new compound of ideas, or a new theory, giving forth, probably, a new vibration! Something has been created, and a little has been added to evolution. One or two people in history, thinking in this way, have produced inventions, doctrines and discoveries which humanity has found invaluable ever since. Consider what it would mean if humanity as a whole were to learn so to think. Civilisation would change out of all recognition.

Because nobody has been doing enough thinking, things have come to such a pass that the only resource of men, after all these centuries, is still war! But fighting will not produce any solution to international muddles and difficulties, nor has it ever done so. The only remedy possible must be one of international co-operation and organisation, planned by the most competent and visionary minds on this earth. These plans must have the support and understanding of a large portion of the general public before they can successfully be carried through.

The solution to the world's troubles will depend, in the last analysis, upon clear thinking by a few, backed up by the intelligent understanding of the many. It is extremely urgent that this clear thinking is developed as rapidly as possible, in order to avoid many more years of wasteful warfare and suffering. The trouble is that man has not trained himself to understand and apprehend the trend of his own evolution. He cannot appreciate the significance of the march of events around him, perceive to where they are leading, and deduce what is to come. He has given progress a mighty push forward, in the mechanical sense, with his marvellous inventions, but then he lags behind in his ancient ruts, clinging to conditions which he himself has buried. This causes an unnatural gap between life as it is, and as it is lived, and results in cross-currents, unbalance and confusion, giving us the state the world is in today. Until man gets free of his mental ruts and opens his eyes to the fast-changing conditions of life, and understands how to move in step with evolution, he will continue to be an unhappy travesty of what he is meant to be. Every man and woman must become a really alive and thinking unit in order to produce a public worthy of a new and grand civilisation. The glorious adventure and freedom which thought brings will open up a new world to them and emancipate them from their present puppethood!

Man acts because he believes that his actions will bring forth certain results. The bird builds its nest because it anticipates in its own way certain family developments. All life looks to the future. Perhaps it is only in ratio with our ability to estimate the future that our life will not be lived in vain.

All the greatest creative works have been achieved well ahead of their time.

Primitive man plans for the next few hours.

Average man plans for the next few years.

Superman plans for the coming centuries.

The urgent need, therefore, is to learn to see what is ahead of us, *if that is possible*. I believe that it *is* possible, and that, without the aid of astrology, prophetic dreams or psychic visions, but purely through a logical thought process, we can tune in the mind to that part of its own world where the plan of the universe and the process of evolution is mapped out. It is, I am convinced, a process as practical, as scientific, and as sure as that of using a wireless set. The difficulty we have to contend with is lack of training, lack of inherited tendency and lack of practice. Yet even in spite of these handicaps we shall demonstrate in this book to what astounding revelations and inspiring propositions we can penetrate, solely through learning to control the fractious steed we ride upon—the mind!

Such an experiment, however, must obviously be a very difficult one, or its results would have been given to us long before now. In order successfully to carry it through we must be able to launch our minds out from their accustomed harbours and set sail upon the boundless ocean of life's mysteries. We must cast overboard everything except the barest essentials, throwing away every preconceived idea, every habit of thought, even those conceptions which have always seemed simple and obvious truths, plain and apparent facts. Sometimes there is nothing so utterly deceiving as a plain and apparent fact! This is because one is apt to forget that life is all change and movement, and that which is a fact one moment may not be so the next.

When a pupil of the Zen Buddhists wishes to attain wisdom through Meditation he is first taught to throw away all his most intelligent ideas, all his profoundest and most rational questions, until his mind becomes like empty fertile earth ready for the planting of new impressions. We cannot hope to achieve this empty-mindedness, the work of many laborious years, without such expert training. But at least we can remind ourselves constantly that the mind must be open if anything new is to gain an entrance!

The temptation, when seeking wisdom, usually is to move backwards through time, leaning upon the work and the words of the ancient thinkers, making their time-worn theories our own, and then proceeding to feel possessive and satisfied about our secondhand knowledge. This may enlarge our viewpoint, but our coming experiment requires more than that—it requires that we do some original thinking, produce some modern deductions of our own. Therefore we shall only take the barest glance into the past, just enough to touch upon certain outstanding landmarks in the progress of man's development, up to the present day.

A comprehensive view of history will give us an impression of recurring periods, cycles, tides and waves in human affairs. Life has ever been so, and it will doubtless continue to be so—

history repeating itself, but always with a *difference*! It is that difference, that newer element which forever enters in, that constitutes evolution, and points the way to the future.

As our object is to ascertain the moral and mental progress of man, if any, we need not turn our attention to the vistas of wars, conquests, and rising and falling empires, which stretch back into the endless reaches of time. We must seek deeper, and try to define changes and modifications in the human being of everyday life. In this way we may discover clues to the trend of evolution during the past, and noting the particular lines along which that development moves, we can follow it through to the present day and use it as a pointer to the future.

Average man has always presented the picture of a curious mixture of good and evil, of brilliance and stupidity, energy and sloth. This amazing ensemble is perhaps not quite so inconsequent as it may at first appear. Psychologists have declared that every virtue has its complementary vice. Apparently a little too much stress on some particular aspect of a virtue transforms it into a vice. By the same token, therefore, any human vice either in a nation or in an individual exists because of its tendency or capacity for a certain virtue, its power being capable of transmutation into that virtue. For instance, virtuousness itself can so easily change into priggishness, authority into tyranny, subtlety into deceit; just as meanness may modify into thrift, pride into dignity and laziness into serenity. All the virtues are interchangeable into the vices, and the very strength of a vice shows the possibility of an equally strong virtue. It is a subtle margin which heralds the switch-over in many cases.

As we study the growth of human character during the fraction of its history with which we are familiar, it is well not to be dismayed by outstanding bad traits and habits, but to realise that in measure as they grow so also grows their reverse side, the virtue, although it may remain for long in abeyance.

Man's first primitive instinct was surely that of self-preservation. Even before he learnt to inhabit a cave his first thoughts must have been how to protect himself from wild beasts and other dangers.

Secondly, he acquired a mate and a few articles essential to his needs, and his guardianship extended to these also.

Thirdly, he discovered that it was a good plan to train his children to be useful to himself, and so add to the strength of his home.

Thus we find that self-preservation, possessiveness, the wielding of authority and the use of propaganda were respectively the earliest traits developed in man. These traits took such deep root that they are still the guiding-rein to his actions, in spite of the profound changes that have come over his world since those early days. Science and social life have transformed conditions on this planet so that self-preservation and possessiveness need actually no longer play much part in the forming of character. This world could now be organised so that men need never go in danger from each other, and can, if they so will, enjoy the possession of the whole earth together. As for the wielding of power and propaganda, it has been shown to be far more practical when equally and wisely *shared*.

Nevertheless during thousands of years those earliest traits in man have moulded history and have produced fundamental underlying instincts which still largely rule our ways.

Self-preservation has resulted in that widespread effort to acquire for the self, if possible, more than its fair share, whether as an individual in doing business for 'profit', or as a nation seeking territory and 'trade balance' without care for the needs of 'rival' nations.

Great efforts have been made through the institutions of religion and of law to curb man's acquisitiveness. Were it not for these restraining influences we should surely see a world of unbridled banditry and bullying.

As it is, profiteering, usury, and the acquiring of an unfair share of possessions have been steadily carried on in ways which have not been too crudely obvious to a public growing insensibly accustomed to them. In time the average decent man has been bludgeoned by social conditions into a readiness to make his profit without considering who is the loser by it.

Far worse than this, the obscene outrage of war has flourished mightily during centuries of effort and progress, due to humanity's primitive pugnaciousness and separative tendencies. Man's earliest brute instincts continued to stalk beside his every achievement. As soon as he began to appreciate fine virtues he tried to run them in double harness with those baser impulses. He seemed afraid to raise his head and clearly see the need and the possibility of letting go his ancient habits. He had a very strong conservative urge, and although he was ready to take on the new, he tried to cling to the old at the same time.

Thus when magnificent new religions were raised up they were soon made responsible for as much cruelty and evil as virtue. Patriotism, another fine attribute, has been responsible for acts of heroism and acts of barbarism alike. The qualities of enterprise and energy have resulted in profiteering and self-aggrandisement, as well as in improvements. Scientific discovery has added always to the unhealthy and dangerous in life, in measure as it has given comfort and entertainment.

Men have achieved marvels of art, culture, science, organisation and invention. They have shown irresistible patience, devotion, courage, inventiveness and love of beauty. Yet alongside of all this, vice and stupidity have kept even pace, with the result that, in the mass, life continues to be lived mostly in want, in fear, in drudgery, in ill health, in ignorance, and in danger of complete annihilation by one's fellows.

In spite of many intermissions, these conditions have been recurrent. History has presented this picture as a whole right up to recent times, a picture of incoherency and illogicality.

Now surely the mainspring behind all of life is MOTIVE, this being determined by the point of view, and the sense of values.

History has shown us, therefore, that the fundamental *motive* and the sense of values possessed by mankind up to now must somehow have been both mistaken and unpractical.

Should not the motivating force of a man's life be suggested by his religion and strengthened by his government?

Let us glance quickly at the simple rules laid down so definitely in the Christian doctrine, and embodied as well in all the great faiths which were planned to produce an ideal social life.

Man is commanded not to kill.

Individually, he is punished by the state, for its own protection, for so doing, but encouraged and obliged by the state, when it chooses, to make a glory of collective slaughter!

He is required to have as much love and care for his neighbour as he has for himself. But neither individual nor nation has yet learnt that all well-being depends upon the equal well-being of all.

Religion teaches that if anyone asks for his coat he is required to give his cloak as well! These instructions still sound fantastic to him, they are so opposite to his habits of profiteering and possessiveness. Yet if *everyone* gave away his things to those who needed them everyone would still have enough, and possessions would be more equally distributed.

Lastly, men are asked to answer force with gentleness. This seems to them impossible as 'it would result in their being over-run by tyrants'. A little thought will show that no tyrant could or would care to rule the world for long—it would mean far too much work, and the fact of having no opposition would reduce him to only taking what he really needed. Naturally these remarks are open to a flood of argument. Let us wait first until we have enlarged our vision somewhat.

Up till now humanity has been divided in its motives—seeking to ride two horses, the one steed representing religion or ethics, and the other the ancient instincts of greed, fear and self-aggrandisement.

The result is a community where the flower of man's genius and the beauties of his achievements are of small account in a life of strain, want, muddle, incoherency, ill health and imminent danger.

All the glorious annals of history have so far led only to this

—a world which could by now have become a paradise, and is instead an uncomfortable chaos! This may sound exaggerated, but that is because we are so used to the chaos, and cannot visualise the paradise.

Our glance at history has shown us a world in which men, although they have made great efforts to curb their own evil tendencies, have not found the clue as to how it can be done. From time to time there have been periods when slaughter and persecution flourished, and periods when art and culture flourished, and periods when healthful living and social reform flourished, and periods when spiritual ardour and religious faith were especially strong. Like a see-saw, vices and their virtues have taken turns to come to the top, sinking just after they have reached their peak.

Men have eternally striven to produce a fair and fertile land, fine cities, and beautiful estates. They have put incredible toil and ardent inspiration to the making of magnificent buildings, palaces, monuments and art treasures of a thousand kinds. They have given their wealth and their homage to religions, superbly housed, which forbid them to take life, to oppress, to ravage or to steal, and teach them to worship gentleness, beauty and justice. They have dwelt under governments whose expressed purpose was to build up a system ensuring safety, order and good living. In these ways have men striven to achieve happiness and prosperity.

And then?

As a very crown and peak to these achievements they have enthroned—WAR!

War has been glorified, fighting has been upheld as the greatest thing a man can do for his country.

War!—which entails murder, destruction, ravage, oppression, robbery—is thus diametrically opposed to all that men have striven to build up, and in a few hours can render matchwood, ashes, corpses, cripples, and waste-land of their whole existence!

What an insane, illogical, ridiculous state of affairs! Men have thus been brought up in a world of such crass contradictions and irrelevancies that clear thinking has been inhibited. There has been only one attitude for the average man—that of blind and traditional compromise.

Thus as clear straight thinking has been in the way and unwanted it has dropped out of use. A man did not say, 'Either I am to follow my religion simply and truly, or I am to obey the behests of business and of my government which are diametrically opposed to it! If I am to be a genuine human being I cannot do both!' Instead he endeavoured somewhat apathetically to please all sides, and to mould his thoughts to fit this double life. Thoughts so fixed became static and sank generation after generation into insurmountable ruts. The result of this was a type of mentality which put the public at the mercy of mass hypnotism and propaganda.

Communities, being made up of such individuals, also grew into set patterns, producing nations which, while claiming complete authority over all those within their bounds, yet refused to acknowledge any authority themselves. The more obedience and peaceableness they exacted from their citizens, the more they demanded for themselves the right to invade, destroy and rob their neighbours. Such nations have gone by the name of 'sovereign states', which sounds well, but in actual fact means that the state as an individual unit is nothing but a bandit!

There are instances throughout history of wonderful efforts to overcome this condition of national banditry. Some of these attempts have met with encouraging success. Neighbouring states and principalities have agreed to drop their sovereign authority, or share it, as in the case of Switzerland or America. Our historical review, which carries us up to the end of last century, thus finishes on a note of promise.

Nevertheless traditions die hard. The kidnapping of a people by a stronger people has been held up as glorious empire-building! The kidnappers have said: 'We don't approve of the way you live, and you and yours will be useful to us, and it will do you good, so—we take you!' Later on, having thoroughly established the usefulness, and taught the people to live along their own lines, the kidnappers say : 'It is possible that if you continue to live exactly as we wish, and to be useful and friendly to us, we will grant you a measure of self-determination and self-government.' This is all made to sound very noble, and no mention is heard of the tremendous addition in wealth and strength which such action has brought to the kidnappers. Still, it is in a certain sense the relinquishing of banditry, and is therefore promising.

It seems that self-interest has been the automatic mainspring of life up till recent times. Every man for himself, every country for herself, every class and creed for itself. This has resulted in a thousand little antagonisms, bound together to resist greater antagonisms. Throughout many centuries man's spirit has found no escape from those conditions, and has been unable to pierce the shell of habit and tradition. Within these limits he has achieved much, but it has brought him little joy.

He has created many ingenious and beautiful things, but thought has been at a discount, and his mind has been pushed into the dimmest recesses of his being, hidden over and forgotten.

So much is this the case that it is unrealised even by some of the more intelligent of us today—which makes it necessary in the proceeding pages carefully to prove how little are people acquainted with the art of thinking, and to essay to lift the curtains which veil the forbidden territory—our minds!

Our brief consideration of man's history showed us a succession of marvellous though disconnected achievements, scattered throughout a life which seems dislocated through lack of coherent thought, and reduced to a chaotic mixture of building and destroying, sense and nonsense, inspiration and idiocy.

Unil the end of last century people seemed perfectly complacent about it !

5

An Approach to Discovery

SEED THOUGHT (SECOND STAGE)

We have considered the story of man up to the beginning of the present era, which we may roughly place around the commencement of the twentieth century. It is possible to recognise the change into a new era by certain marked differences. At its inception we found a leisured world, in which the art of home life, of culture and conversation, of intense class consciousness and of settled self-satisfaction, both individual and national, were the general characteristics.

During the last fifty years, however, enormous changes have taken place. Science has come into its own, remaking social life in many ways, speeding things up and bringing one complication and difficulty after another in its train. Science has cast a network around the earth, filaments of intercommunication by land, sea, air and ether, which have drawn the world rapidly together, making of it one small interwoven whole. This has happened far too quickly for a humanity so embedded in its antagonisms and separatisms. People have been flung out of their attitude of comfortable security before they have discovered what to put in its place. War and brigandry has continued unabated, but now everything that happens is known immediately by the whole world, and can be discussed between those at one end of the earth and the other while still taking place !

This means that even the lowliest peasant can be world-conscious. Because of the tremendous progress in the newspaper world, because of the rapid development of the radio and television, he can from his humble cottage follow step by step everything that is happening all over the globe. He is being steadily dosed with information, with propaganda, with music and with entertainment from early morning to after midnight.

Thus the mental side of humanity, as a whole, is beginning to come into its own at last. To be well informed is now the prerogative of the many instead of the few. Class-consciousness is still present in the educational system, and plays its part in company with party politics in the daily press. But with radio and television quite new factors have come into being. They give out the same to beggar and to duke, as they speak to all the world. They ignore and negate class barriers, and any sections of their varied entertainment are liable to appeal to any type of person. They have one audience, composed of everybody! They are actually the first educational body (when regarded in that sense) to adopt this attitude, and this is an extremely important innovation which has passed with little notice.

Thus science, although blamed for many recent social difficulties, has in reality performed an inestimable service in drawing humanity ever closer together and promoting understanding and sympathy between all peoples. This of course has been growing for some time. People have been awakening to a feeling of responsibility for every member of their kind the world over, irrespective of nationality. Charity has extended its vision from home to abroad, until today it is about as easy to raise funds for a little-known people at the other end of the world, if they are in dire need, as for urgencies in one's immediate surroundings.

All these changes have come about without attracting much attention, but they are significant and profound changes, nevertheless, and they are changes which are *new in history*. Wars have come and gone, empires have risen and fallen, but this welding of the world into one communicating family is a grand new brand new achievement, which must herald the coming of a different kind of civilisation altogether, so soon as the present muddles have been cleared up.

For other reasons also there can be little doubt that we are living in the most pregnant and vital time in history. There is another thing happening now which has never happened before. The whole world is gradually dividing into two camps. On the one side are those who believe in living by force, theft, persecution and cruelty. On the other side are those who hold that such methods are obsolete, and who are standing firmly for liberty, justice and gentleness. The latter side are largely the Christian side; at any rate their attitude constitutes an approach to the Christian spirit; whereas the former camp is definitely anti-Christian in both its methods and its declarations.

Caught between these gradually forming opposing forces the rest of humanity are being drawn to take one side or the other. They saw the middle of the century dawn upon a world tensed and anguished. They are shaken out of the makeshift complacency of former years, and are turning anxious eyes in all directions. They are confronted by the spectacle of a world ridden by terror and slaughter, disease and want, injustice and cruelty, unemployment and malnutrition—and all this as the result of their efforts and success in science, agriculture, labour-saving devices, rapid transport and intercommunication! In spite of magnificent achievements for the improvement of living conditions, the seat of human trouble remains uncovered, the spirit of progress appears to be playing a losing game, and this fair world seems to be imminently threatened with complete moral and economic collapse and retrogression.

The tempo of living has been so rapidly speeded up and concentrated that these facts are now self-evident and urgent and their realisation is running through all grades of society. People are beginning to see that comprehensive and drastic action must be taken, not only to win several more wars, but to set civilisation upon new and safer foundations. This desperate need is at last becoming apparent to all and men are ready to confess their failure to run the world. The crucial moment is therefore drawing near when, if there were a sound plan put forward to rebuild international conditions of living, it would have the attention not only of a few enlightened minds, but of most of the general public throughout the world.

Of what does this general public of the twentieth century consist? With what aggregation of types have we to deal?

I think we can roughly divide them into three classes.

First there comes the simple type which we might call 'animal man', meaning nothing derogatory in any way, as we are most of us far below the animals in their own sphere. That sphere is the home of what we call 'instinct', and therefore 'animal man' is he who is ruled by instincts. These primal instincts are those of self-defence, of feeding, of rearing a family, owning a home, and enjoying the simple pleasures shared with animal life. Among the animal instincts are many of the noblest, such as mother-love, heroism and devotion to one's own, bravery and patience and industry and energy, all concerned with the bare necessities of living. A very large number of human beings belong essentially to this first class.

The second class into which we can divide mankind we can call the 'human man', one who has associated himself with those things which belong essentially to the race of men, rather than of animals. The outstanding characteristic of the 'human man' is self-centredness. His life is moulded by this instead of by instinct.

Self-centredness entails self-expression, self-aggrandisement, and therefore emotion and feeling. Man discovers himself as an artist and creator of beauty, as a possessor of power and property. He needs an audience and he becomes gregarious. This results in social life, in its battles and in its beauties and in the world as it has existed hitherto. The 'human man's' attitude to his Deity is that of a child. He continually asks for more, and for help. He is lovable in the way that a child is lovable. He lives for entertainment, beauty and comfort, and self-expression. He lives for himself and for those people and things which contribute to his happiness. If he is convinced

that God contributes to his happiness he will try to live for
Him a little too.

So we have the second class of mankind, a fluctuating mass,
ready to be influenced for good or for bad.

The third class is by far the smallest. We can call it that of
the 'idealistic man'. Such a one is he who has become detached
or decentralised from his own personal interests. He is ready
to share his success, his work, his credit; he is co-operative,
and it is from those of his type that the longed-for 'brotherhood of man' could be formed. He is of the spiritual as opposed
to the material calibre. He feels responsibility for world conditions. He is not possessive, is not violently attached to his
home, his family or his nation. He has lost enjoyment in
antagonisms and rivalries. His attitude to Deity includes a wish
to serve Him and to understand His purpose.

These three types have existed since early times, although
often somewhat mixed through so-called heredity. Of late
more and more examples are to be found in the last category.
These three classes represent three phases of evolution. We are
just entering upon the third phase.

During the long story of the past man has been governed by
his emotions. In the fine man this meant sentiment, in the lesser
man it meant sentimentality. It gave us fanaticism and it gave
us devotion. The world was ruled through men's conceptions
of their religions, into which they put all their separatisms and
antagonisms.

Gradually, however, the age of science has come upon us.
Here sentiment and emotion have no place. A man-made
Deity has no place either. The God worshipped is truth and
fact, and for this we ought to be glad, for surely He can stand
the test. Men's eyes will be opened and they will see Him as
pre-eminently the God of science, of order and of plan.

Science has been giving us a new material world to live in,
and a new moral world too. But so far, although during the
emotional phase of history men have been ready enough to con-
nect beauty and art with Deity, they have not so connected
science. Scientists are not revered as holy men devoting their

lives to uncovering the mind of God! On the contrary, man has been apt to think himself the prey of science, because he has not yet learnt satisfactorily to deal with the forces and potentialities which it has unleashed.

We have been passing out of the age of emotion into the age of mind. This is a great event in history because it is the first time it has taken place. It heralds a fundamental change in civilisation.

Certain people have subconsciously responded to this change already. They have tried to escape from old ruts, from tradition, from convention, from everything in fact which belongs to the past. They have given us 'modern' art, music and literature, freedom in sex life, and even a recoil from ancient courtesies and manners.

We have seen also the first germs of a widespread desire to use the mind. The newspapers mirror this for us, with their crosswords and other puzzles, and their voluminous correspondence, and other contributions from the reader. It has become a slogan that 'everyone writes nowadays'. A vast quantity of people have published literature of some kind. The fact that public interest in astrology came to stay points also to the subconscious belief in geometrical forces at work in the universe.

Another significant and recent development is shown in the vast number of groups and fraternities with 'Utopian' ideals which bid fair to honeycomb the life of the people. All these groups without exception point to the 'dawn of a new and golden age', but whereas up till recently they were mostly confined to religious and psychic communities, they have now begun to invade the thresholds of political and economic reserves. A Utopian future in world affairs is no longer held to be a glorious impossibility, or even probability—it is now seen to be a necessity!

The Arts have always been universal and have bound men together the world over in common appreciation and pride. Science also knows no barriers, its honours and conveniences being shared by all without thought of nationality. It has been

in religion and politics that man's baser instincts of antagonism and separatism have flourished, thus letting down the
whole fabric of civilisation through the exercise of wrong
motives and sense of values.

There are promising signs of late that this insuperable
stumbling-block has been realised by the people, and that steps
for its removal are being taken. Such movements as the United
Nations, World Federation of Faiths and Federal Union would
hardly have been possible years ago. Now they arouse echoes
on every hand. The world has begun to feel blindly for
unity.

These are the questions in everyone's hearts just now : 'Are
people awakening to these needs and necessities in time? Is it
possible to pull humanity out of the morass in which it is
foundering, and can we learn to read and understand the
forces which are moving underneath outward human manifestations? We can see the effects, but how might we learn to
estimate the causes? Is it hopeless to expect a Utopia, or is it
close upon us?'

These are the vital questions which need answering. We
shall attempt to answer them during our Meditation, having
now set the stage for our mental exploration by a brief survey
of the conditions leading up to it.

In the great age which is just passing, the age when religious emotion ruled the world, men quite rightly sought for
inspiration in their hearts, and an interpretation of life in their
religion.

In the new age which is now upon us, the age when science
and the mind will rule the world, men will quite rightly seek
for inspiration in their minds, and an interpretation of life in
their scientific discoveries. This is not to put aside religion, but
to make it one with science, which in fact it is. And this is not
to put aside the heart either, but to clarify the riddle which
Christ spoke : 'As a man *thinketh in his heart* so is he.' So far
men have used their hearts for feeling, not for thinking. This
is the most basic form of separatism, and the cause of their
irrational duality.

According to our assertion, then, man's next task is to learn to interpret the message and purpose of Deity as it speaks through science. The upbringing of humanity during its long adolescence has been accomplished through the emotions. But now it is about to reach maturity, and, becoming responsible, will be able to stand truth without sentiment—a truth that is vast, impersonal, awe-inspiring, and lies pregnant in the domain of the mind, expressed in the so-far uninterpreted language of science.

It will be our endeavour to decipher this language, and thus uncover the plan of world development, the process of evolution, and the stage of this process which lies before us in the immediate future.

6

The Secret Language of Science

CONCENTRATION (THIRD STAGE)

The mystery of life, the trend of existence, the stupendous secrets which lie locked from our view behind the gates of birth and of death, send out their silent challenge with the radiations of every star, and on the hushed breath of space itself.

Throughout the passage of time a hundred mighty minds have wrestled with the secret of their own existence, and have explained, propounded or denied the mysterious source of themselves, and of all around them. The statements of these great thinkers stand out like scattered stars in the dark sphere of our worldly knowledge, some pointing to the north, and some to the south, some giving a big light and some a small.

Space and time, force and matter have been the subjects of vast numbers of theories, hypotheses and declarations, many of them brilliant and intriguing, but most of them apparently in disagreement one with another. The ancient savants explained life in terms of planes, the modern scientists work in terms of vibrations, while our most advanced thinkers postulate in terms of dimensions. If we could ascertain what these terms actually signify we might discover points of resemblance between them. Possibly, when gathered together they might be made to form a coherent whole which would cast a clearer light upon the mystery of our own composition, the purpose of our existence, and the manner in which that purpose is being carried through.

As we are going to try to formulate some original theories we will avoid all contact with ancient thinkers and savants for the present, as well as the spheres of poetry, religion and philosophy in whose language they expressed their genius. Instead, true to our concept that the present age is being pre-eminently ruled by the scientific aspect of Deity, we will seek to read the Divine message and lesson as it is instilled into this world through the medium of science, confining ourselves for awhile to the realm of scientific conceptions.

Perhaps the highest peak of modern scientific thought of this century has been achieved by Einstein with his little-understood Fourth Dimension. As most of us have no pre-conceived ideas about this seemingly abstruse subject, it will provide a suitable starting-off point in our search for the secrets of the universe. Do not let us be put off by the word 'Dimension'. We have chosen it in order to keep the train of our Meditation in 'modern' terms, and to prove that it is not necessary to borrow the language of the Eastern mystics nor of the Western Bible in order to penetrate the mysteries of being. We shall avoid the use of scientific terminology also. No matter how involved or difficult a subject may appear to be, I believe it is always possible to describe it in short and simple terms, in clear straight phrases which can be understood by clear straight minds. Our trouble is that some of us have lost the habit of straight clear thinking. We are inclined to meander around, we conclude beforehand that certain sub-jects are beyond us and would not interest us; we shy like wild ponies at unaccustomed thoughts; we twist and turn rather than quietly face new ideas. We are liable to gape at long-winded scientific postulations, allowing ourselves to be hypno-tised into stupefaction by them. The average intelligent person is, however, able to understand a vast amount more than he might expect to do, provided it is put to him clearly and shortly, and his own mind is attentive and quiet. I have as proof the profound change I have been able to effect in my own mentality simply because I realised how well worth while would be the effort. Once the mind is cleared, it is annoyed by the amount of involved verbiage in which essential facts about life are wrapped up.

Mr. Einstein made mountains of calculations and figures around his Fourth Dimension, which acted as an impregnable fortress against the average mind, and isolated his work completely from human life. A few specialists appreciated his discovery and gave it the celebrity which it deserves. Yet who understands the value of his work? Who uses it? What are those same people who acclaimed it doing about it?

For the very reason that it *seems* so unapproachable and unpractical I suggest that we think around Mr. Einstein's discovery until we tune in to the secrets which lie behind it. We can best build up our approach to this Fourth Dimension by first considering the lesser dimensions in their respective order.

The word 'dimension' comes from the Latin *dimensio,* meaning a measuring. The initial practical human reaction to things is to find out their size and shape. This can best be ascertained through measurement. The first measurement is simply the shortest distance between two points, and gives us the straight line. This corresponds somewhat to the FIRST DIMENSION, which is merely the first elementary movement through space in one direction only.

The consciousness of a creature living a life of one dimension could be compared to that of a blindworm stretched straight along the ground, immovable! The first-dimensional consciousness could not be aware of space at all, except on a flat surface, and moving in one direction only. First-dimensional existence expressed the primal urge or push forward of life.

The second dimension is found when a line or direction can be taken at an angle to the first flat plane or straight line. We then find other shapes coming into existence, such as the cross, the square and the triangle. We now have two directions, but so long as movement can be made in two directions only there is still a flat surface, our two measurements giving us its length and its width. The important aspect of two-dimensional life would be that of intersection. Two different lines of force, two opposing currents meet. They may intersect, cross each other, or fuse. Interaction of some kind must take place, which was of course impossible with only one dimension. Such interaction must necessarily be either attraction, repulsion, or fusion. In either case a certain amount of cohesion must be produced. For it needs cohesion even to resist. So that the second dimension would express the second primitive urge towards life, that of attraction or cohesion. The artist and the draughtsman have to work in only two dimensions, that is to say upon a flat surface, and their art consists in expressing three dimensions when using only two.

Once cohesion is established a centre or core is formed, and around this centre a form takes shape. A centre or core can attract or repulse in *all* directions, so that at this stage life has become released from the flat surface, and can produce solid objects, and the THIRD DIMENSION. This third dimension or measurement gives the thickness of our subject, so that with length, breadth and thickness the dimensions of all physical life may be ascertained. The sculptor works in three dimensions.

If the distance from the core of an object to its surface is the same in all directions the result is a ball or globe. Therefore in the third dimension the curve is born, and circular movement, or rotation, is demonstrated. At this stage an object can rotate or move in all directions, through all the angles. The third dimension, whose scope includes the first two, covers all motion and all shape in the physical world. It gives us the rotating sphere, and therefore the atom, the planet, and the solar system, and all the life which is built up from these. Therefore, after the primal urge, the push forwards, the WILL to live of the first dimension, followed by the ATTRACTION and cohesion due to the second dimension, PHYSICAL LIFE appears in the third dimension as rotation and vibration.

This trinity of dimensions corresponds to the Holy Trinity, in which there is the first aspect of Deity, WILL, the Father, the primal urge; the second aspect of Deity, LOVE, or attraction, the SON; and the third aspect of Deity, the 'Mother' or the Holy Ghost, Spirit crystallised into physical life and manifesting therein. For we must not forget that all is Spirit, physical matter being Spirit at a lower rate of vibration. As the scientists put it, all is *energy* in the last analysis.

So, during the earliest stages of our train of thought, even the simplest of the dimensions are acquiring a deeper significance, and are linking up with powerful forces.

We can class the lower three dimensions as belonging together in their expression of the outward physical side of life; and as it is the third dimension which actually produces form, we shall refer to all three dimensions in future under the heading of the Third Dimension.

During many thousand years the human mind has been intensely productive in everything that belongs to the third dimension. The Fine Arts and all the amenities of living are the results of the efforts of the human spirit to express its inspiration in the world of form. All further possibilities were the monopoly of the poet, the dreamer and the philosopher, some of whom met their chance by forecasting many of the inventions of the future to an incredulous world. The artists and architects of those days were often scientists as well, and their work was the greater for it.

Are we able to read the message in divine language which the third-dimensional life expresses to us, and the lesson which humanity has had to learn from it? It is the lesson of materialism, the dealing with and the conquest of solid matter. The law which governs it is the law of Separatism. Physical life expresses itself by means of infinite divisions and separations, forming ever-increasing numbers of isolated objects, their isolation being caused by the fact that in the lower dimensions of form life each object requires its own space, and there is no interpenetration.

Man has learnt the lesson of Separatism extremely thoroughly; in fact it has become ingrained in him. Under its sway he has produced multiplicity in all his activities. His ideal has been to have many things, not few. His speech has become ever more complicated and full of words. His possessions and needs have become innumerable. His architecture and design degenerated from simplicity to fussiness of detail. Science, which has been *one* science, and a necessary qualification for all the leaders of men, guarded faithfully by the priesthood itself, became split up into a dozen sciences, each one going off in splendid isolation, until at last we find identical things masquerading unrecognised under various names.

Separatism finally gained utter sway, and man's earlier recognition of the unity of all life faded completely from his memory. It was the era of self-development, of extreme egotism and intense sacrifice to the three dimensions. I am speaking now of the great passing chapter of human existence, which to most of us embraces all we know of history. At times during this period art has reached marvellous heights, and material living symbolised by home life has been beautiful indeed. Unfortunately, however, the more man concentrated upon the third dimension, the more he became separated from his hitherto involuntary recognition of and awareness of the higher dimensions, which we are going to explore. He came in the end to adore his physical world and live only for what it could give him. As most of this consisted of solid objects which could be taken from him, greed, possessiveness, love of power, the inclination to take for oneself at the expense of others and the readiness to tyrannise were the results growing out of this unbalanced adoration. His character became marked by extreme egocentricity, and his activities made for an ever more complicated existence, with an increasing infinity of divisions and sub-divisions, each fighting to retain and increase its individual strength and draw all sources of supply unto itself.

This type of life produced greed, fear, the stronger preying upon the weaker, and finally despotism, when men began to come together under one leader. The wiser of the tyrants would care well for his possessions both of men and goods, in his own interests. The feudal system, as we knew it in England, was built up under this influence. The chief or lord acquired sovereign authority over all his land and people.

The invisible strings of evolution pulled! The lords came

together to a larger merging, counties and departments were formed, and later little states, which still embodied the spirit of possessiveness, aggressiveness and sovereign authority. Later a further merging took place, and nations appeared, which flourished through an even larger measure of acquisitiveness and sovereignty.

Actually the merging process was the first herald of the future death of separatism, but we have to take a very long view indeed to appreciate these vast epochs. Hundreds of years will have passed ere man works his way entirely clear from the experience and lesson of the third dimension.

Let this short indication suffice us for the moment, while we move on to different realms, always keeping the association in our minds between the lower dimensions and physical life, the arts and crafts, possessiveness and despotism.

7

The Fourth Dimension:

The Fourth Dimension was acclaimed as the great discovery of the century by those who had the authority to pronounce such a verdict. Unfortunately its advent has been at a time when human beings are still struggling so desperately to gain ascendancy over the first three dimensions that they have no strength left with which to contemplate the existence of a further one. They leave it to the scientists, as something which could have no significance for the ordinary man and no possible connection with the swiftly changing conditions of life around them.

In fact, the mere act of living seems to have beaten mankind. He appears unable to cope with the question of his own health, being less competent in that respect than the animals. He lives in a wonderful world of plenty, yet his economics are so poor that he is less successful in his management than the white ant. He complains that in his social and international life the jungle law appears to rule. Crime is no longer the prerogative of the criminal—it has become the orb and sceptre of some of the leaders of men.

While all the time longing for joy and for peace, men are yet made to spend their livelihood in manufacturing instruments of wholesale slaughter for use upon their brethren-in-distress! In their desperation they are inclined to blame 'science' for their troubles.

Let us consider whether they have any justification for this.

Perhaps we can ascertain the actual significance of this mysterious Fourth Dimension, and the inventions connected with it.

Many of the discoveries of this century have been active in a realm outside and apart from third-dimensional or so-called physical life. They have dealt with substances which are neither solid, liquid or gaseous—substances which can neither be seen, measured nor weighed. Of such a type are all electrical appliances, like the telephone, electric light, radio and many other inventions which make use of radiation. To this list can be added the many known rays, such as X-ray and ultra-violet ray, which are now in use.

The harnessing of electricity and the harnessing of sound-waves for the use of radio or wireless have opened up a tremendous new world to thinking men. It has been realised that the machinery of human beings is run and kept in action and fed with the requisite energy units by electricity (or by forces still put under that one heading). Messages from body to brain are carried by 'electricity', and the same phenomenon produces the resultant action. In like manner electricity plays a leading part in the life of an atom or a planet.

Let us see if we can define the fundamental difference between electricity and the many other invisible phenomena which we call gases, and which we admit to be physical because they can be resolved back into both liquid and solid form. One of the outstanding points about electricity is that it appears to be impervious to the law of gravity which holds the three-dimensional world in bondage.

This law of gravity is the magnetism which emanates from the earth's core. Every living body exercises a law of gravity to a certain degree. The earth is held in the sun's orbit by the latter's emanation of gravity or magnetism. It is gravity which determines and restricts the rate at which solids, liquids and gases move, according to their weight and density. In comparison, electricity is free of this bondage. It can travel almost any distance at a pace which to us seems instantaneous. It can penetrate through solids, and it can move in all directions. This capacity brings quite new factors into our calculations.

Time and space exist for us as such by reason of the fact that in three-dimensional life all solid bodies must be placed in juxtaposition. Progress amongst them must be made on or over their surfaces at the rate at which it is possible to cause the respective progressors to move. This terrible sentence means, more simply, that because of a person's particular weight and energy plus the law of gravity, his movements take a definite length of what we call time. For the same reasons the earth takes a portion of time which we call a year to move round the sun. Time and space are more or less fixed quantities in the three-dimensional world.

But when the factor of moving energy, or electricity, enters in, quite different conditions are to be found. The universe is composed of two substances, energy and matter. 'Electricity' is a term which has been applied to certain aspects of energy with which we are familiar, but let us bear in mind that at present we are using the term very loosely. Energy and matter are in a constant state of interaction, interplay and inter-changeability. A human being is actually energy dynamising matter and moving it about. If we wish to put it more fully we can say that a human being is a complexity of various subtly graded degrees of energy, which dynamise and move about a complexity of various subtly graded degrees of matter. The different degrees are determined by different rates of vibration or oscillation. The exact place where the subtlest matter ends and the 'coarsest' energy begins would be practically impossible of definiton. We will realise that the same statement applies to our earth, after we have studied the atoms which compose it and their relative constituents of energy and matter.

This energy or electricity is everywhere, moves through all the universe in every direction, and can be located in earth or air. As soon as man was able to put it to his use he became much more independent of the law of gravity, and therefore of time and space. For instance, if we telephone to those living in Australia, they receive and answer our remarks twenty-four hours earlier (to them), and we realise that we have overcome one day in time, and the width of the earth in space. If our earth was twice its size and rotating at the same speed, and we telephoned to Australia, would they not receive and answer our remarks forty-eight hours earlier (to them), thus overcoming two days and twice the distance? If our earth was as big as the sphere of the solar system would not the same experiment overcome a year of time? Would we not receive a reply from people who are busy living a year ago?

When Einstein worked out things like this mathematically he proved that time and space exist only in accordance with the weight and size of the object concerned and the distance from which a viewpoint can be taken. A person walking on the ground will take approximately one minute to cover fifty yards. If he were to rise up a few hundred yards in a balloon he can look down upon all that space and be in command of it, so to speak. He can descend again at equal speed to any portion of it. If he ascends in the balloon to a height where his viewpoint covers one mile, which would take a quarter of an hour to walk, and leaves a friend down below to walk it, he is then in a position to see ahead of his friend in both time and space. He can prophesy what his friend will meet along the road. He has overcome the normal restriction of space to a small degree. But he has not overcome time, because he has to use time to ascend and descend in the balloon.

Supposing, however, that instead of ascending, our experimenter remains upon the ground and sends a television camera up in the balloon, from which he receives a picture. He can use it to obtain a bird's-eye view of the road ahead. The higher he sends the balloon the more hours ahead he can see upon the road. In this way time and space have been overcome in a small degree through the bringing into use of the fourth-dimension quantity which we call 'electricity', or energy.

We noticed that the law of gravitation and the third dimension seem to be linked together. We first linked the third dimension to the motion of rotation which lays the foundation for physical life; the law of gravitation (or the cohesive pull at the centre of a sphere or body) is of course interdependent with it.

Permeating and influencing these motions of physical form, yet comparatively untrammelled by gravitation, and able to flow in all directions throughout the solar system, are a vast number of what scientists call 'rays'. Many of these have been located and their qualities determined, but a huge number remain undiscovered. Some of these rays are built upon a gigantic scale and come to us from outside our solar system, and these have been named cosmic rays. All of them appear to be intimately associated with our 'electricity'.

It is apparent that these rays with their various electrical constituents must be playing through the body and brain of every human being. We have reason to believe that mind and memory are electrical in nature, or at any rate exist in or use the electrical world. It is by reason of this that mind can act independently and outside of the physical body. Because mind is able to travel at the speed of electricity, and can at times play the part of our television camera in the balloon, it can sometimes see ahead and 'prophesy'. The manner in which this is done is outside the scope of this chapter and has been considered in my earlier books.

To continue with our train of thought, it appears that the fourth dimension could be described as that world of subtle matter invisible to us, which is outside the laws governing solids, liquids and gases, which latter phenomena hang suspended or embedded in the ethers. This brings us to that much-abused word—*ether*. We are told that this is a kind of invisible material which acts as a carrier to light, sound and electrical waves and apparently fills all space. Inasmuch as man is beginning to take a definite cognisance of its existence and character we can call it a physical manifestation, and suggest that it is a grade subtler or finer than gas. It is already being questioned whether ether itself is divided into definite grades of fineness. We have been into this question before,[1] when we noted that ancient savants postulated seven states of matter—

[1] See *The Finding of the Third Eye.*

solid, liquid, gaseous and four ethers. Modern scientists are already convinced of the existence of more than one ether.

The fourth dimension may be said to apply to those states of existence which function and move through the fourth state of matter—the ether! But this statement must be made with reserve, as being only temporary. Because if there are four ethers, possibly the fourth dimension may not function in all of them. I would suggest here that we consider the existence of a fifth dimension, in which might be found activities motivating the finer ethers not yet located by modern science.

Certainly it is the ether or ethers and their functions and possibilities which have been exercising scientists and inventors of the present era, as well as the various rays which play through them. Ever since the discovery of rays and radiations and electrical energy they have been working with fourth-dimensional matter and with fourth-dimensional laws.

We saw that the manifestation of the third dimension is continuous curved movement in space—rotation, which embraces all other angles and movements, and that it is under the law of gravitation and the restriction of the physical aspect of time and space.

Now we must define the manifestation of the fourth dimension. We can name this as radiation, expressing a movement which we can call 'throughness', as opposed to tht more specific surface-covering movements belonging to the first three dimensions. Radiations pass outwards in all directions from large bodies, such as suns and planets, and are absorbed, modified, and re-radiated outwards again from all smaller forms down to the atoms. The fourth dimension gives passage to the electrical and other life forces which feed and imbue the concrete form. If a man could picture himself as having his consciousness functioning in the fourth dimension, he would be able to see in every direction at once to any distance, and cover all space with the speed of electricity. Time and space would no longer exist for him to anything like the same degree.

Let us now consider whether man has, indeed, any actual personal relationship with this fourth dimension. He contains within his body every mineral and element which go to make up the physical world. Every form and feature of plant and animal life are traceable within him, too.[1] Beyond this, he also claims a share of the ether world, or world of energies, as part of his make-up. Through him pour all the existing rays and currents. If, therefore, he, containing matter of the first-, second- and third-dimensional worlds, can move in, utilise, and control that matter exterior to himself, it is logical to suppose that, containing also, as he does, fourth-dimensional matter, he should be able to move in, utilise and control that matter also. This would imply the capacity to see and feel substances not classed as three-dimensional, but of a higher vibration than physical, in other words, superphysical or supernatural. It would include also the power to travel in time and space with the fourth-dimensional or electrical part of a man—his mind—at fourth-dimensional speed. We see at once that many of the so-called psychic gifts must belong in this class, such as clairaudience, clairvoyance, prophetic vision, and long-distance vision. We shall consider these more fully later on.

The possibilities of the fourth dimension have begun to be capably exteriorised in such developments as television and wireless. But the fact that man is and should be capable of performing interiorly and of himself anything which he can cause crude metals and machinery to do has not yet been grasped. It is just about to be realised that the power of the mind actually to wield and affect matter is a scientific fact. I believe that it will not be long before interesting developments in this direction take place. Meanwhile psychology is approaching ever nearer to the forefront of medical science.

Let us now see whether we can uncover the message, read the secret and divine language, and appreciate the lesson which is given to us through fourth-dimensional life. It is a world of radiation and re-radiation, continuing until every living emanation is passing through, interacting with, blending with and mingling with every other emanation—until nothing is any more separate!

[1] See *The Initiation of the World*.

Fusion, blending, unity, interdependence, interaction, are shown to underlie the deceptive separatism of outward physical life, giving it the lie—showing that the separatism of form life is a delusion, for it is based upon and springs from the utter fusion of rays which are as chemical and solid as physical objects, only more finely divided in atomic respects.

The fourth dimension teaches us that the nearer we approach to reality, to the source and cause of things, the less does separatism or isolation exist. Therefore separatism takes us ever further away from our connection with realities. Separatism is the expression of our limitations under physical vibrations. It involves us in ever deeper complications, and moves always away from simplicity and coherency. It has been necessary for man's conquest of physical matter and material living, but it acts in direct opposition to his understanding of his next task, which is the conquest of the fourth dimension, and the adaptation of his living to the world of fusion and radiation, wherein nothing is separate any more. It is this great change of outlook which is the message of the fourth dimension—the death of separatism, and the return to the oneness of all things. It is this lesson which humanity is struggling to learn or alternatively fighting against, a lesson diametrically opposed to many of its ingrained thought habits. It is the lesson of unfocused universal love, a love which does not differentiate or prefer.

From the fourth-dimensional world one secret after another is being revealed and given to humanity for the better learning of this lesson. Telephone, wireless, television, all these marvellous inventions which knit up human beings in the closest intercommunication; the study of radiation, even of the grand cosmic radiations which link up every star with every other star; all are pointing to the unity of life. This planet has become recognisable as one organism, in which the nations play the part of organs; they live as members of one family, as fractions of one whole, and the passage of events is proving to them their underlying interdependence.

It is because men do not and cannot understand this inevitable development as yet, that they cling to their old habits of thought, strengthen the walls of their prisons and keep their pride of national sovereignty, of personal religion, of family and possessions, fighting to the last mental ditch to remain within the blinding confinements of a separative life.

The fourth-dimensional world calls to humanity to be free, to inherit the earth and the skies, to own all things, to enjoy all things, and, through love and unity and radiation, to understand all things. It impinges ever more strongly upon human consciousness and human activities, drawing men like a steady and colossal magnet from out of the prison of flesh and form, fear and isolation. It seeks to switch the focus of their lives into another realm of being, giving them other values, other ambitions, other standards and other enjoyments. It seeks to prepare them for a still more amazing phase of evolution which lies far ahead, but is drawing all the time nearer—the rule of the coming FIFTH DIMENSION.

8

What is the Fifth Dimension?

CREATIVE MEDITATION (FIFTH STAGE)

The fact that there are now acknowledged to be four dimensions should be enough to make any thinking man question:
'Well, what about a fifth dimension—where is it?'

Having brought our train of thought up to this point we are now ready to meditate upon this question of the fifth dimension.

We have been considering life as it has been built up through a series of dimensions, from the first to the fourth. We cannot yet say which of these dimensions was the first to manifest, or whether they all began to function simultaneously. As the fourth dimension appears to be the one through which the actual life forces play and by means of which they reach concrete forms, we must consider it the most causative or influential of all of them. It represents the nearest approach we have made to the life imbuing all things. But this last and inner dimension has no boundaries; it stretches formlessly in all directions—it is everywhere.

This gives us an incoherent, inchoate condition to picture as the basis lying behind physical structure. It does not give us much clue as to how things take shape. We must next consider, therefore, the question of that principle in life which gives things form. We began with a line, continued with the cross, and on reaching the third dimension we had accounted for squares, cubes, triangles, circles and globes. With the fourth dimension we had radiation, which enables these different lines of force and angles to meet and intersect, producing these forms.

If we can try to picture the atmosphere around us as it would look if we were able to see all the forces, currents and movements as they continue in perpetual action, crossing, circling, spiralling and radiating in every possible combination and in every conceivable size; and if we could imagine each of these currents as leaving its own visible little track in the air; and if we could in imagination watch this process long enough, we should soon have seen outlined every one of the beautiful forms in mineral and in plant life. We should have seen crystal, leaf, snowflake and petal sketched in.

Properly to visualise this picture, however, we must first realise how many trillions of stars, constellations and solar systems are throwing out powerful rays in all directions, which are re-radiated again from every stellar body they strike. These rays are each one of different mineral composition, and each intersection of any two or more of them must produce chemical reaction of a differing quality. Besides this, every rotating star cuts through these rays in circles, or rather, because of its forward movement, in spirals. If we furthermore remember that the subtle constituents of all these radiations are actually the same as those of which the earth is made,[1] we can begin to feel that the life which is playing through all space is really a tangible, clear-cut and definite manifestation, which would appear much more crowded and intricate to our sight than our everyday physical world. These constituents are infinitesimal particles of all the mineral kingdom, which have been radiated out or have escaped from the periphery of the atoms which make up the physical world. They include ions, electrons, alpha and beta particles; little bodies which are propelled at colossal speed through the air, partly because of their light weight, and partly because of the stupendous force which palpitates within every atom. Take a few million of these dancing particles, condense them together in right relationships, and you have a microscopical speck of physical matter.

[1] See *The Initiation of the World.*

Yet all these mad little particles are dancing along the radiations to produce predestined interaction between star and star, moon and plant, sun and man. They are dancing the dance of growth and evolution, dancing into the patterns which make up sound, form and movement.

Having shown what countless designs can be made by the interplay of all the cosmic currents, our next move will be to try and discover whether there are any proofs of their being actually so made. Let us consider, therefore, how the frost patterns take shape upon a glass window-pane. They appear out of space before our eyes. They were not formed by third-dimensional means, they were neither made by hand, nor grown out of cellular life. The fourth dimension, being formless, could not have made them. They must, in fact, have been there all the time! They must have existed in that portion of space, in all space, perhaps, only requiring a window-pane upon which to crystallise, a window-pane whose thickness is a fraction of an inch.

Another point to consider is that if frost is formed on the pane while the sun is veiled it takes fern-like shapes, such shapes as the earliest vegetation of the earth showed while this planet was still shrouded in thickest mists. But if frost forms while the sun shines upon it, rose-like flower forms appear. Both these alternatives were there all the time—in the same fraction of space filled by the window-pane. How many other forms are lurking invisible in that same slice of air, inter-penetrating each other and yet still independent?

Let us remove the window, and in the same space place an instrument called an eidophone. It is like a megaphone, with a drum stretched across the large end, and it is held with this drum upwards. On the surface of the drum paste is spread. If a few notes are sung into the megaphone the paste will form itself into designs, geometrical in character. And if, instead of the paste, a powder be used, tree-like figures will appear.

In these ways we can prove that there are innumerable invisible shapes in space, permeating each other, and yet differentiated and answering to different vibrations of sound, heat or cold. These forms can apparently be located at any point in the atmosphere, by producing the necessary conditions. Possibly they travel upon the radiations of the fourth dimension, and maybe we shall later have to accustom our minds to consider design and radiation as inseparably connected. But at present we can only conceive that these designs do definitely exist in the atmosphere and that this can easily be proved.

When we can get to grips with this stratum of the universe, this sphere where designs come into being, we shall, I believe, be at home in the FIFTH DIMENSION.

Whereas the quality of the fourth dimension was formlessness and continuous radiatory movement, one single motion in all directions simultaneously, that of the fifth dimension is quite the opposite. It is poised, held, concreted, dense. It is the contrary movement to radiation, it is interpenetration, wherein worlds can dwell one within another, remaining quite separate, and even unconscious of one another.

Thousands of people have seen 'ghosts' walking straight through walls, furniture or people, without apparently any conscious contact being made. Are these beings which exist in that same 'invisible' but definitely concrete state as the uncrystallised frost flowers? Might there not also be other entities passing unconsciously through the 'ghosts'? Is it not feasible that in this particular stratum of existence, this malleable fifth dimension, exist the prototypes of all form upon earth?

We can begin, then, rather cautiously, to postulate the fifth dimension as that state of manifestation wherein any number of bodies, entities or shapes can exist in the same spot. If several smoke-rings are blown from various directions into one place a faint simile of this may be illustrated. But it is a poor simile. We have to learn to imagine that myriads of shapes, probably some familiar to us and some not, are peopling the atmosphere more densely than anything we know of in physical life. Where these forms come from, whether they exist in different grades or strata, and to what they are attached are questions with which we must grapple later.

Scientists have stated that they can ascertain the number or rate of vibration of a thought, and that several thoughts of a different wavelength can exist in the same space without influencing each other. Anything in existence which has acquired an individuality, such as a cell, an atom, or even a thought, proceeds to send out radiations. It has become like an electric battery, which draws its own wavelength from the cosmic radiations, sets up its own rate of oscillation or vibration, and by this means re-radiates energy again, energy coloured and differentiated by its own individuality. Each of these myriad individualities has its own pattern or form. We can see the design of a cell by means of instruments, but as yet we have no instrument to show us the pattern of a thought. It will come.

The wireless has taught us that a melody or a spoken word can radiate outwards all over the earth and be picked up at any number of spots by a suitable receiver. Every word that everyone speaks, every sound from bird or beast, radiates outwards as well. The eidophone, of which I have just spoken, can show us the shapes which these sounds make, the original shape built up, through which the energy was poured.

It appears to be clear that the design comes first and the radiation afterwards. It is the pattern which inaugurates the vibration. So we are right in allocating form to the fifth or innermost dimension in our efforts to unearth ultimate causes. We may suspect that the fifth dimension contains the design, pattern and plan of all which takes shape and place. Therein dwells the mind of the universe, the artist and the architect of nature. Once the design is there, in this mental invisible state, we depend upon the fourth dimension, that world of living moving energy-radiations, to pass these designs through into physical matter, to disseminate them and to bring them to life.

The fourth dimension is therefore the link between mind (ultimate mind) and matter. It is the vehicle, the carrier of the design, the idea. Finally physical matter becomes the vehicle, the carrier and the embodiment of both the idea and its energy, of both the fourth and fifth dimension. It is interesting to make an analogy here again with the esoteric teachings. The astral body of man is the body of energies and emotions, and is said to be the vehicle of the mental body. The astral plane corresponds in many ways to our idea of the fourth dimension, whereas the mental plane, the mind sphere, named the fifth principle, corresponds to our fifth dimension. The esotericists teach, however, that there are seven planes or spheres belonging to man's universe, so at present we must reserve our definition of where the fifth dimension really begins or ends. It is difficult enough to imagine this unseen world surrounding us, with its countless millions of radiations playing through earth and air in every direction and all the time. So soon as we are able partially to realise this picture we shall visualise human beings and solid objects as *comparatively* immovable concretions or crystallisations poised in a world of scintillating, shimmering motion. When we further understand that all the rays and radiations composing this world are coloured—latterly even the colours of thought-waves have been demonstrated—the marvellous beauty and complexity of the life around us which we are as yet unable to see will stir our imagination.

In the midst of this palpitating invisible world hang the designs and patterns which mould our life. We have to consider whether these designs are propelled along the rays to which they belong, or whether they exist along the whole length of the rays, like the pattern in a stick of London rock. In the latter case our imagination could not compete with the actual condition because the ray is not like a stick, but radiates in *all* directions.

In any case, the designs are there, everywhere. There they persist, remaining utterly unchanged and unaffected by storm, tempest, heat and cold, wind, cloud, sun, light and darkness. All the latter conditions are superficial, superimposed upon that rock-like foundation of design and pattern, which fill, locked within and within each other, every fraction of that which we call space.

Space so far has meant for us an area wherein a certain

quantity of shapes, gases or substances is able to be packed, or arranged in juxtaposition. It allows for movement in all directions, around and through these substances.

Space is something which stretches out and is full of places! While movement is something which proceeds from place to place! All this is fairly straightforward until we have completed our study of the fourth dimension.

But as soon as we find the necessity for a fifth dimension and begin to understand where its implications are leading us, we have to admit the existence of entirely different conditions and begin to do our best to imagine them. Instead of a space which stretches we have to consider a space which *condenses*. Instead of shapes and substances being in juxtaposition or permeation, they are illimitably contained in one spot —IN ANY SPOT, and IN ALL SPOTS! Instead of movement from place to place we have movement of great force which does not proceed from place to place but is everywhere able to be tapped—a kind of movingless movement, which can best be described as reserved force or WILL.

The fourth dimension was described as *throughness*. The fifth dimension can be described as WITHINNESS. This means that the cause of every growing thing, the form upon which it is built, the force which holds that form intact, and the energy which causes it to grow are not factors which come from outside it, from some other part in space. They are all welling up from that tremendous dimension of withinness— the FIFTH DIMENSION—which will not be understood by humanity as a whole for many hundred years.

Each dimension, as it becomes discovered, understood and applied, gives us the use of greater forces. The unthinking man would consider that a stone hatchet was of more strength than one of gaseous substance. Let him watch, however, the way in which an acetylene blowpipe cuts through metals—even under water, where his hatchet would be quite unwieldy. When fourth-dimensional forces are used they are able to master anything in the third-dimensional world.

The fifth-dimensional forces, whatever they are, should be

more powerful than any of the others. We have already observed what terrific force must be active to hold a design permanently in the atmosphere immune to any disturbances or conditions. The force of fire is strong, but it is susceptible to many things. Electricity depends upon movement, it has to come from somewhere and to go somewhere, and it gets used up. But this mysterious fifth dimension seems to belong to quite different laws and conditions. The designs are there, immutable, immovable, held there by the primal force of creation. They are independent of movement, or of modification.

Another point to note is this. Inasmuch as we find the design of a fern or a tree prolonged through space, we must consider that the design of a human body may be there also—perhaps in a different degree of crystallisation, or rate of vibration, perhaps depending upon other forms of 'frost' or sunshine to bring it to visible solidification. Before man invented a glass window-pane he could not see the frost flowers; he would have denied their possibility. Assuredly later on he will invent another type of surface upon which other 'archetypal' forms will congeal. We will consider what steps have already been achieved in this direction later on.

Meanwhile a study of the fifth dimension has shown us three things: (*a*) the fact of designs running throughout the atmosphere; (*b*) the fact that several designs exist independently in the same space; (*c*) the supposition that it is the original design or individuality which sets up radiation and sends forth rays; and (*d*) that there is a tremendous force behind all this holding it in manifestation.

Let us now consider if we can find any analogy to these activities within, for instance, a human being.

We will take at random one of the many strange medical recordings, that of a woman dying of cancer, who was put upon the operating table as a last resource. After commencing to operate it was discovered that the cancers were too numerous and too far advanced for the slightest hope to be entertained, so the surgeon stitched up the incisions without having done anything at all. The woman was due to die, but when she recovered consciousness they told her cheerfully that the operation had been a complete success. The patient made a rapid recovery, to their amazement, and all cancerous growths disappeared.

A few years ago this case would have remained a complete enigma, but today there is more chance of an explanation. So much has been and is being done from the angle of vibrations, and it has been demonstrated that disease and health are all a question of varying vibrations or rhythms.[1] If one can shatter the rhythms at a given spot and impose a new tempo upon them, one apparently causes the protons and electrons to re-collect in differing proportions, forming a different pattern, and a tissue or substance of a different kind takes its place. These results have been obtained by electrical instruments, such as the infra-red lamp, the ultra-violet lamp, the X-rays, radium radiations, and the sunshine lamp, for some time now. In such ways the work which should be done naturally through the interplay of cosmic radiations within a human form has been assisted or augmented. The latest types of healing electrical instruments are those which deal with the radiations of shortest wavelength and highest frequency, thus becoming ever more subtle and delicate.

Many doctors will admit that it is usually impossible to know how much of the work of healing has been done by the instrument and how much has been achieved by the patient himself under his own subconscious collaboration. With some of the latest of these vibrational healing instruments it has been found that in some cases the patient is able finally to do the same work upon or within himself without the instrument! The procedure has been registered by his subconscious mind which now uses his own 'animal' electricity to shatter and rebuild the rhythms in his body. This process has been loosely named auto-suggestion, hypnosis, etc., and no scientific explanation of it has as yet been given. But it does prove that *within* man is a will or force which can act from *behind* the patterns and

[1] See *The Initiation of the World.*

designs upon which his tissues are built, and, changing their rhythms, can bring forth another design *in the same space*!

We thus find a complete analogy with our frost flowers and our five dimensions within the activities of the human form. We have the first three dimensions presenting to us the complete physical person, the fourth dimension radiating all the life, energy and emotion through him, the fifth dimension containing all the myriad alternative patterns which can play various parts within his form, and finally that something behind it all, that will or force which is able to decide the final issue.

We have seen that humanity's first great lesson, that of the third dimension, has been Separatism, in order to master the solid world and emphasise individuality; and that its second great lesson is to be the relinquishing of Separatism and egotism, and the development of love, fusion and unity, under the reign of the fourth dimension.

The lesson of the fifth dimension is *coherency* within that achieved unity. This entails the uncovering of the plan, the purpose and the method of evolution, so that man may work intelligently along evolutionary lines, sensing always the pattern which lies behind each outward manifestation, and tracing all the differentiations back gradually to their one originating source. The lesson of this dimension is that life—the entire life of this planet—must be organised as one complete, coherent and simplified whole. This does not mean the loss of any individuality. Man's body is one integrated whole, yet each of his organs, nay every cell, retains its appointed characteristics, even its own wavelength. The more integrated and orderly is the whole, the more important is the individual original part which each fraction of it must play.

This tremendous lesson of world integration will produce a quite new civilisation, an utterly different mode of life—the life of the future which we will attempt to vision as it will be when ruled by the fifth dimension, after the fourth dimension, which is now beginning to take hold, has had its sway.

9

The Secret of Dimensions Uncovered

Having arrived this far in our definition of dimensions, let us now classify some of the thoughts which have emerged from our meditation.

Are we any clearer as to what dimensions actually are? Has the name come to mean to us anything more than a mathematical symbol?

We have seen that life appears to be graded in a long series of varying states of matter, from the most solid to the most subtle or gaseous; and that ancient savants or esotericists declared these grades to be seven in number, each containing seven subdivisions; they called them planes and sub-planes. The early Christians knew of these divisions and called the subtlest plane of all, in their own language, the 'seventh heaven'. The modern scientist grades his world by its rates of vibration, the lower or slower rates producing 'solid' matter, and the higher or faster rates producing energy or 'electrical' matter and the shortest wavelengths.

The higher mathematician and the architect see their world in grades which they have named dimensions, which appear to be the modes of expression of the different grades of vibrations. So far they have given us four dimensions, but our meditation has already brought home to us the existence of a fifth, and what it is. And the inspiration which comes next suggests that as the link between dimensions, planes and vibrations is obviously so close, if seven is the key-number of the planes of the esotericist and of the vibrations of the chemist, it may also be the key-number of the dimensions. We can therefore suggest that there may be seven dimensions in all.

In accordance with this assumption we may now tentatively state that :

A DIMENSION IS A TERM USED TO COVER THE ACTIVITIES OF PROBABLY A SEVENTH PART OF THE VIBRATIONS INTO WHICH THIS UNIVERSE IS GRADED.

We must not assume from this that all of these seven divisions are equal, to any degree which we could understand. We must also realise that the dividing line between them all is very very subtle and hard to find, and that they are in a constant state of interchangeability one with another, according as rates of vibration are being speeded up or lowered. The principal factor which causes the raising of vibrations is heat, and the lowering of vibrations may be said to be due to lack or want of heat.

If we are right in surmising the dimensions to be seven in number, each inner one more potent than the last, and if humanity is on the verge of mastering, accepting and understanding the fourth of these, then it follows that *only just over one half of the possibilities of man and his world have so far been exploited.*

If we further consider that only one or two of the earliest inventions relative to the fourth dimension, such as the discovery of electricity and wireless, have changed the face of society and the possibilities of living to an enormous degree, we may well begin to question what the discoveries in the realms of the remaining dimensions will bring to us. We must admit that they may bring changes in life which would at present appear as inconceivable as wireless would have seemed a few hundred years ago. If we have only reached the half-way stage in man's progress so far, our final achievement will make us as different in the future to what we are now, as our present state is from that of the most primitive savage.

We are about to see how much we can discover, through meditation, of man's future achievements, and the stages by which they will be reached. As we have said, in the practice of meditation the method is to set out the problem or question absolutely clearly, by means of which the mind is well exercised and concentrated. As soon as the mind has thus been tuned in to the information required that information begins to flow through, just as electricity flows through if you turn on the switch. Information, any information, can be tapped by the mind from its own dimension, and thus be acquired without words or books, according only to the skill achieved in this practice. We will return to this point later, and meanwhile put it into practice by focusing our minds still more clearly upon our subject.

We shall do this by considering just how far modern science has advanced in the uses of both the fourth and fifth dimension, and that will give us a good stepping-off place for our projection into the future.

All those inventions which have to do with radiation and with wavelengths and which use the ether or ethers as their medium are fourth-dimensional. From the time when these inventions were made practicable we have been existing in a fourth-dimensional civilisation. This did not happen suddenly. Everything overlaps, anticipates itself, fades out and reappears during considerable periods of time. For this reason people have been at one and the same time battling their way to the finale of the third-dimensional epoch while already using and improving fourth-dimensional activities; and they have also been making a beginning in studying and anticipating the possibilities of the fifth dimension, even if unwittingly; and although few of its implications appear yet in the observations of modern science, we can be sure that it will inevitably take its place when the time is ripe, and change the face of society quite as radically as the coming of electricity did, perhaps even more so. We can contemplate these changes in a later chapter. Meanwhile it is necessary to bear in mind that much work is being done concurrently in third, fourth, and fifth dimensions, and to keep them clearly differentiated.

Modern scientists have succeeded in analysing, locating, and using an astonishing number of rays or radiations, whose frequencies and wavelengths they have determined, and of whose mineral constituents and especial qualities they know a certain amount. Among these fourth-dimensional activities we must list everything to do with electricity, including telephone, wireless, radio, lighting and heating and electrical energy; plus all the many uses to which rays and radiations are being put, including the violet-ray, X-ray, colour radiations, the radiations of sunlight, and the cosmic rays. Some rays are used by the doctor, some by the chemist, to effect new compounds, some by the scientist to form new synthetic materials; in fact they are put to use in every walk of life, making many things possible which were inconceivable before. Continued research into radio-isotopes and the characteristics of sub-atomic particles is engaging men's minds, and the space programme gives us much new knowledge of cosmic rays. From the finite to the infinite, from the immeasurably small to the immeasurably big, the realm of the fourth dimension is steadily giving up its secrets to the insistence of man's patient curiosity.

We must also take into account not only the external but the internal work which people have been developing along fourth-dimensional lines. Most of this has been classed under the name of 'psychic'. It includes the capacity to react to radiations subtler than those to which the average person responds. Since last century this work has been growing steadily in volume, and among its branches are included the various elements of spiritualism, different types of mediumship, psychometry, healing, clairvoyance, clairaudience, long vision, prognostication, automatic writing and drawing, hypnotism and mesmerism. All these activities and many others come under the domain of the world of radiations, and are attracting an increasingly large number of the public.

The mould of social life as a whole has been recast by the innovations attendant upon fourth-dimension discoveries;

human beings have had to adjust themselves to the different conditions which the employment on every hand of these new factors entailed. Little by little, and almost automatically, people have accepted the fact of the existence of these myriads of radiations. Apart from psychic work, they have not thought much about them, tried to understand them, or apply their obvious inferences in regard to themselves. Vibrations and radiations have been considered to be strictly within the domain of the scientist, and the layman has felt no need of giving them any thought. True, the spiritualists actually have experimented with electrical and magnetic phenomena and gained certain results. But they have relegated all their work into the domain of the so-called supernatural. This has divorced it from orthodox scientific interest, while keeping it, nevertheless, too unorthodox to be received into the domain of the Church.

The Christian Scientists, who also worked with mental radiations, couched their doctrines in terms unacceptable to either the spiritualists, science or the Church.

Thus a large body of facts and data was accumulated in separate compartments which in their turn were cut off from the average thinking man by the labels of sect. We shall consider later what will be the result of removing those labels, and of having only one nomenclature understood and used by all.

We have now observed the extent to which men have already harnessed the world of radiations to their use, and to what degree they have so far conquered the fourth dimension.

We must next study the earliest efforts of science in the realm of the fifth dimension. We must not mind a little reiteration in these chapters. Unaccustomed conceptions need to be repeated until the mind begins to accept an unusual picture. We saw that the movement of the fourth dimension is outwards and onwards in every direction at once—the movement of rays, waves and radiations.

The movement of the fifth dimension is the reverse—it is inwards! We have to get the idea of distance and depths illimitable being traversed while still in the same spot. This at first sounds incredible and unimaginable—but It Is So! It is merely the reverse side of Einstein's picture, the completion of the annulment of time and space. Its understanding holds the key to undreamt-of possibilities.

The forces which traverse physical space, all those fourth-dimensional radiations with which we are becoming familiar, are powerful indeed. They can burn, melt, mould and change matter of lower dimensions than their own. But the forces which dwell within the great WITHINNESS of higher dimensions still, must wield the ultimate power over all.

We have said that a radiation is inferior to its source, and that first of all there must be an original pattern, design or individuality which initiates the radiation; also that the plans and designs for all physical life must be crowding the atmosphere to an extent inconceivable to us in that stratum of the universe which acts as its designer and architect, the realm of the world-mind, the fifth dimension.

To what extent and in which ways are men making use of this realm? The most obvious channel, of course, is the medium of the same material—their own minds. Every idea, inspiration, or 'brain-wave' that a man encounters has been directly picked up from this sea of world-mind matter, by his own small mental equipment; amongst the thousands of rays that are radiating their patterns and pictures through his person in all directions, those that are of a frequency nearest to his own particular tune-up of the moment are reflected and photographed on to his own mental apparatus. We will consider this question of reflection and photography later.

If we were to set out to collect such evidence we should soon find that so-called original ideas, discoveries and inventions are come upon by several people at about the same time; that such people are usually quite unknown to each other and often dwell in lands far apart. Several people, for instance, were hot on the pursuit of wireless waves, but it remained for the one who could put his inspiration into most practical form to reap the credit of discovery. Most inventions are invented by more than one man. Plots for novels have been duplicated, ideas for pictures, inspirations for poems. The best piece of work has lived, the lesser have hardly seen the light of day.

The capture of a mental picture from another person's brain which we call telepathy has also often a close connection with this world of fifth-dimensional design. We must remember how difficult it sometimes is to distinguish between the original design in the fifth dimension and its reflection along the length of its fourth-dimensional rays.

Man is using the fifth dimension for every idea that he acquires. He may use it involuntarily, as most of us do, or deliberately set out to explore it and capture a treasure, as do the pioneers and artists of this world. The mind of the pioneer is sufficiently one-pointed and forceful to penetrate the WITHIN of the fifth dimension to the original idea and design itself, whereas the man of lesser mind simply reflects that which comes to him along fourth-dimensional rays, obtaining the shell rather than the kernel, and obtaining it at hazard.

In such ways then do men already use internally the forces of the fifth dimension. Let us next consider whether externally in science they have conquered any of its domain.

The most obvious instance, of course, is that of television. This proves that objects can project pictures of themselves with the aid of radiations, or, to put it otherwise, can radiate pictures of themselves through the atmosphere. These pictures can be translated from one substance or medium to another by artificial means so successfully as to be comparatively unchanged. Photography itself proved that the shape of an object is projected through the atmosphere in all directions so definitely that it will impress its own picture or image upon any receptive surface.

The latest inventions and discoveries are proving very much more than this. According to their findings it is now claimed that every *individuality* impresses its own image upon the surrounding ethers, which image may be captured by suitable photographic instruments.

Let us get quite clear what we mean in this case by an individuality. We are using this word to cover any object in the universe, solid or non-solid, which has its own self-insulating vibration. By 'self-insulating' we mean a vibration or frequency which is separate to itself alone, and which cannot be dis-integrated by any other individual vibration, nor by heat or cold. Such an object may be a tiny cell in a human body, an atom, the form of a thought, a human being, an animal or a planet.

Each cell in a human body is an individual, with its own especial frequency, differing from any other in the world. But the human body as a whole vibrates to its own ultimate self-insulating frequency, which rules over and colours and flows through all of its cells. The photographic image of the human being as a whole is impressed upon the ethers around it by the vibrations or rays which carry it outwards. These rays flow through every one of its cells, which each reflects and holds the photographic image in its microscopic dimensions. Each atom of the cell receives the image and holds it in the dimen-sions of its own ultra-microscopic sphere. Then one and all continue to radiate their images and frequencies out into the world.

These radiations are fourth-dimensional and electrical. If a small portion of the body is separated off from the whole and removed to the other ends of the earth the link is never broken so long as life remains to the individuality. The portion is linked strongly to its owner by the self-insulating frequency, which acts as a 'private telephone and television wire'.

We have earlier considered the work of Dr. Ruth Drown, who has apparently claimed, brought forward and proved these theories through her remarkable inventions; we also spoke to Dr. Lakhovsky, whose wonderful work has uncovered much of the world of radiations to us. Several more splendid pioneers have been working at this time, each approaching from a different angle to prove the same truths.

There is not space here fully to go into the thrilling work such people are doing, but we can sum up their findings as follows :

Every individuality projects an image of itself along the

length of its radiations. These radiations emanate from the governing oscillation, pulse or frequency of the individual, which is unique and self-insulating, and rules all lesser vibrations within the whole, which latter are impressed with both image and frequency. Therefore the picture or image of any individuality can be recovered from any fraction of the whole, which has been removed to any distance from its source. Once in possession of such a fragment, a line of electric communication is established, and messages and impressions can be sent along it to its source as well as be received.

Once in possession of a drop of the patient's blood, no matter where the patient may be, Dr. Drown claimed to be able to be in such close communication with the patient that she could take his temperature, his diagnosis, a photograph of the part in question, and send healing electrical vibrations to the patient via the drop of blood. Apparently the photographs so obtained varied in size according to the energy of the radiation along which they travelled.

According to Dr. Drown's findings, a goldmine appears to possess a certain individuality, because from a tiny grain of gold images of its source may be obtained. Those of us who are familiar with the 'psychic' gift of psychometry will note here that it is apparently about to be explained and verified by orthodox science. This is happening one by one to all the 'supernatural' capacities.

Another very interesting point brought forward by Dr. Drown was her claim that all living tissue which goes to make up any one organ is governed all over the world by its one key-vibration. The tissue of the heart of emperor, whale or fly has the same frequency and something of the same design; while the tissue of the liver in any creature has also its own especial numbered vibration. This calls to mind the fact that in astrology every organ is said to be ruled by a planet, in a system which applies to all living creatures. If we further remember that each planet is said to control and radiate a certain mineral or mineral combination this becomes more significant. The famous Dr. Abrams and his successors have done much spadework in ascertaining the frequencies of the organs and tissues of the body both when healthy and when diseased. These frequencies always tell the same tale wherever they may be found.

It is perhaps not so very difficult for us to imagine that all those objects with which our eyes are familiar are radiating their images outwards and that the atmosphere is therefore teeming with these moving pictures. This, however, is not the whole of the matter. We have to realise that there are very many existing forms with which our eyes are not familiar, either because they are too small, or because they do not take shape in solid matter. The experiments of Dr. Pfeiffer brought light to bear upon this stratum of design. This clever pioneer produced a crystal of copper chloride into which he inserted a tiny drop of blood. As the crystal forms the blood traces a definite design within it. The design varies according to whether the patient is healthy or diseased. The healthy blood forms a certain leafy pattern, whereas various diseases each produce their own design. The blood of mice also gives the same results. By this means diseases may be detected before any of the usual symptoms are showing. In these experiments the hidden lines of force at work in the ether, which produce such effects as frost flowers, have been put to use. The pattern which is radiated by an 'individuality', such as a definite disease, has been captured in its flight outwards.

We have now touched upon a few of the instances in which science is using and penetrating the fifth dimension. Many more will occur to us as our train of thought develops.

How far have we got with our penetration of the mystery of dimensions themselves? It is becoming clear that, far from being a simple expression of measurement for the architect or artist, or an abstruse abstraction for the higher mathematician, dimensions can be considered as a practical and useful every-day means of understanding, classifying and learning to control the laws and mechanism of the world in which we live. Under the heading of dimensions we can marshal and assemble the little-known array of facts, laws and statistics which have been collected by various studious minds in many walks of life. Perhaps when enough of these have been placed together they will slowly reveal to us a completed picture which will bring revelation. At any rate, I think we can already see that a very intimate relationship may exist between dimensions, planes, frequencies, so-called matter, and some of the sciences such as psychometry and astrology.

There is one further point which comes to mind. For some while scientists have been studying the power of the atom. They have attempted to harness the vast store of power that can be released from its inner core. Where could this tremendous store of power come from? Could it radiate through the atom on fourth-dimensional rays? No, because the characteristic of the fourth dimension is the movement of rays through and onwards, and such forces certainly do play through an atom. The power, though, which the scientists have unlocked resides *within* the atom, always in a state of active immobility. *In reality it is perhaps the atom which resides within the power, being a minute crystallisation in that cross-section of life which we call time and space.*

Perchance the atoms of this earth and all that they form are but frost flowers upon the mirror of life, witnessing to the vast intricate moulding forces playing in all directions, and only certain of the many shapes are caught and crystallised by the mirror at this particular time.

The great force residing within the atom must not be confused with the fifth-dimensional realm, which latter is only the realm of pattern and plan, the *mind-realm*. But the force underlying all things is something different again. It is surely an expression of that WILL to be and to grow, that mighty strength which pushes evolution forwards and yet holds it in place, a force which we must relegate to some higher dimension still.

As we uncover, by means of scientific discovery, the dimensions one by one, the secret lesson of each is there waiting for humanity either freely to interpret and learn it, or to be beaten into it by the inevitable march of events and changes in conditions. The dimensions represent vast major epochs in the history of man, definite stages of experience and evolution. In spite of these succeeding epochs, the dimensions are there all the time, inextricably interpenetrated, showing the ultimate oneness of all things. They each have their part to play, constituting perhaps—the Seven Ages of Evolution! They follow the laws of being, even the law of unbalance which created the physical world—for one of them must always be wielding major power over the rest.

10

How Evolution Proceeds

CREATIVE CONCLUSIONS IN MEDITATION

Let us now consider how evolution passes gradually from under the rule of one great dimension to another.

We have built up before us a vision of a new type of plan upon which the living universe is constructed. We have visioned seven dimensions, representing life expressed in seven classes of vibrations. Through the release and use of energy these vibrations or frequencies can be altered and speeded up, therefore shifting any phase of life into a higher dimension.

For instance, the plant takes carbon and other raw mineral elements, and produces a release of energy through atomic interaction between them. The result is an alteration to higher frequencies, and subtler combinations which produce the sugars and salts of cellular life. Man consumes the plant, and in his turn blends these sugars and salts, producing among other substances the energy he uses in thinking. By this process the original mineral elements have been so subtilised and their vibrations so heightened that they have reached a gaseous state and pass out into the air upon the delicate radiations of man's aura. Through these means a comparatively inert crystallised piece of carbon or other element out of the earth has been liberated and transmuted to a state where it has the freedom of the air and can be radiated from planet to planet.

The process of change whereby any substance can be speeded up to a higher vibration and thus shifted into a subtler dimension is called TRANSMUTATION.

The opposite process, whereby any substance is reduced to a lower vibration and thus shifted downwards through the dimensions towards solid matter, is called crystallisation. For instance a man gets an inspiration from the highest dimensions. He works out the idea and plan (fifth dimension) and imbues it with the ardent energy of his heart and passion. It has now become so cohesive that it radiates electrical energy and has crystallised a vehicle of fourth-dimensional substance, known as a 'thought-form'. Finally it becomes possible to produce it in terms of the lower three dimensions, and it takes shape as some inspired work of art, of literature or of science, having crystallised into solid matter. Thus a divine message or inspiration must be clothed in matter of all the dimensions before it can be expressed in earthly life, whilst a crude chemical element from the earth must be transmuted upwards by man into the dimension of thought so that it can be used to capture an inspiration! The inspiration is then crystallised downwards again into solid matter and expressed through the use once more of mineral and vegetable substances. This continuous cycle shows us the interdependence of spirit and matter, and the interchangeability of energy and solid. It shows us' above all the peculiar power which the mind wields, in acting as a link between the upper and lower dimensions, and in producing interaction between them. This cycle of interaction must be continuous or else the current of life is broken and disintegration sets in. When a man grows old his body and brain become set and crystallised, thus drawing apart from his personality and mind—the side of him which works always towards transmutation. When the gap is too big to be bridged separation or death takes place.

It is this process of TRANSMUTATION which spells the secret of evolution.

All vibrations are in a constant state of change, mostly the change of transmutation from a lower to a higher frequency, resulting in the change from something visible to invisible. Man, animal and plant progress in ratio to this transmutation, which varies from a process so slow as to be imperceptible to one which is quite easily distinguishable, such as that of radium and phosphorus.

In the world of chemical science most operations consist largely of forced artificial transmutations, brought about in many cases by the application of heat (or higher frequency).

By this means the lower, heavier, more inert chemical vibrations of solid atomic compounds are 'split up', changed, rearranged and transmuted to other forms, which usually pulse at a higher frequency, and therefore have become more potent forces with which to achieve effects. The first primitive achievement along these lines was to turn water into steam power, but that is only a picturesque simile of what we mean, because the water itself was not changed. The production of gas out of coal is a better illustration, and many more will come to mind.

Transmutation, then, is one of the major concerns of all scientific activities. It is actually the speeding up and the accelerating of a natural process. It is the externalising into machines and instruments of some of the processes which take place naturally and more subtly in man, animal and plant. The whole earth is actually in process of transmutation. The heavier and coarser elements are gradually disappearing, and in their place new ones are appearing higher up in the octaves of frequencies, but with corresponding numbers.

Thus the earth as a whole is becoming hotter, lighter in weight, and of subtler and more potent material, and the frequencies of all it contains are being steadily speeded up. It is a question also whether this process is confined to our planet or is taking place in the entire solar system. The process is slow and subtle, and scientists are still considering this important problem. When they come to more definite conclusions they may be able to make some strange forecasts of the changes likely to take place in the dim future.

In mankind itself this process of transmutation is slightly more apparent. Humanity is very definitely increasing in sensitivity, and becoming ever more highly strung, 'psychic', nervous, refined, mentally active and complex.

The general transmutation of the planet is greatly helped out by all living things upon its surface. They each exist by reason of this process, obtaining their growth and warmth through the disintegration by various wonderful chemical processes of the coarser substances of the earth and the invisible substances of the air, and their blending to form more highly specialised and complex patterns for the tissues of plant, animal and human life. Up the scale of being the transmutation appears in ever more subtle and potent form until we can no longer follow the trail it blazes before us.

It is man himself who contributes the largest share of the work of transmutation of all that composes this planet. The substance of the mineral, vegetable and animal worlds which pass into his body are amalgamated and fused to form a subtle energy which is electrical in character and which is used to work his own unique instrument, the mind, with its creative activity and reasoning power—those invisible potencies which he alone in nature possesses. In him the transmutation can take place at greatest speed. Its results pass outwards from his body in constant streams of fine electrons, whose mass has been given various names, such as the 'aura', and whose radiations, of the nature of 'wireless', are able to encircle the earth.

What is the answer to this phenomenon of transmutation?

It is that everything is being resolved back into its source, the inner mind-force of nature, and that mankind is the principal instrument of this process. Life proceeds with a continuous cyclic movement through matter and through time; beginning as light or life force, it crystallises into energy or heat, then into gas, then into liquid and lastly into solid. The cycle continues as the solid is transmuted back into liquid, gas, energy and, finally, light. Each time this cycle is completed, however, there is more light and less solid, that is to say more high-speed vibrations and less low ones. This is because the higher dimension or frequency must always rule and overpower the lower one, and this is a law which we must always bear in mind throughout our meditation. It will lead us to a vision of the future. It will allow us to realise that mind can always rule matter, and that will can rule them all. A man *can* think and be as he wills, in all essentials. But real will must be used, and not the fragmentary apology for will which most of us know. We must remember, also, that it is the will which directs the mind, and its pattern-forming work, and that this is often done without the cognisance of the relatively low-frequency brain.

This planet was developed into the form we know through a long period of crystallisation, whose phase of greatest density, solidity and lowest frequency was completed long before life appeared upon its surface. With the coming of organic life transmutation began, and a slow process of reversal commenced, so that for aeons now heaviest physical matter has been disappearing. It is gradually being reabsorbed back, first into the realm of fourth dimension through the radium-like activity of the mineral and vegetable kingdoms, then into the realm of the fifth dimension of archetypal design (maybe we could make the animal kingdom responsible for this if we knew more), and finally to that realm of will and purpose directing inspiration which is peculiar to man, and whose radiations are of the highest frequency of all.

It would be interesting to reckon mathematically, if it were possible, the actual numbers of ions and electrons so far released by man's mind upon this planet as compared with the slower process achieved by other kingdoms. It would also be of significance to note the radiatory effect produced by a man of high and positive mentality as compared with an average individual. The electrons emanated by very potent types have at times been visible to human beings and have been given the name of a halo or nimbus. Modern science has even been able to demonstrate and photograph the coloured radiations of the mind, so we are dealing here with accepted facts.

Let us now see how our picture of the universe is shaping. We have our seven dimensions, within which are classed our seven grades of matter with their various subdivisions. We have the eternally moving cycle of life which progresses through all these grades in spiral fashion, causing interaction and interchangeability, crystallisation and transmutation, its spiral character being evinced by the upward urge into ever higher frequencies, because of which the lower frequencies are gradually passing out of existence. This spiral action, which has been named[1] Epigenesis, proves to us that progress and evolution is inevitably taking place. It proves to us also the fact that physical life is much more intangible than we may have thought, that it is hard to draw the line between life, matter, thought and energy. Everything is liable to be changed into everything else, and our so-called solid earth is verging on a state of complete flux.

Now the question arises as to what it is that prevents that state of flux from taking place? What force or law is it which holds this vast array of vibrations each to its rhythm, and each in its place, allowing just so much interaction and no more? What is it, indeed, which keeps solid matter in manifestation and in existence at all, preventing the rapid disintegration of the physical into its component parts, and holding the complete edifice of the universe to its slow course?

The answer to this question lies in the word POLARITY. The electrical energy which is the essence of all matter is divided into two kinds, positive and negative. In any individual, such as a cell or an atom or a human being, these two kinds are never quite equal. They are for ever striving together to equalise themselves. The core of this battle becomes the magnetic pole which runs through every living thing. It is the urge of life expressed physically by what we know as electricity. An atom has such a pole, so has a planet, and so has the solar system. The rays or lines of force which produce these poles play through the atmosphere in all directions, and in all degrees. They meet, and interrupt each other, because they are never equal in strength. These two unequal opposites of positive and negative, meeting in the air, cause a pull or a 'strain' in the ether. Around that 'strain' they swirl, forming a little vortex. The vortex whirls, and an atom has been born into the

[1] By the Rosicrucians.

physical world! The formation of the atom has depended upon the inequality or unbalance of the meeting forces of positive and negative electricity. The quality or nature of the atom depends therefore upon the respective number and arrangement of the positive and negative electrons (particles of electricity) composing it. The positive electrons go to form the proton or nucleus, while the negative electrons swirl round within the periphery of the little vortex, as the planets swirl round the sun. Those on the outermost surface are subjected to the pull of everything outside the atom, and sometimes they are released. When an atom loses one of its electrons radiation has taken place. The fate of that electron may be to unite or join forces with another unit of a subtler nature than its late harbinger, in which case it joins the rhythm of a higher frequency. An atom is now formed of a more potent type, probably in a higher dimension. Transmutation has taken place.

Transmutation is therefore dependent upon a release from polarity, and polarity is due essentially to a condition of unbalance or inequality, electrical in character. We can thus state that the crystallisation of forces into visible physical matter is due to the existence of electricity in two aspects, positive and negative, which rush together in an effort to unite and fuse, but do not succeed because of inequality in strength. The result is the formation of atomic matter. If the positive and negative charges were to become equalised, fusion would take place, and the neutralised electricity would vanish from our ken, the solid be no more!

Now what relationship does this process of transmutation bear to the evolution of the human race as a whole? What is the secret message of its silent language, and how do its activities co-operate with the dimensions themselves?

The process of transmutation releases units which have been confined to the lower vibrations of atoms forming heavy solid objects, and enables them to come together in higher vibrational groups forming objects or substances of more diffused and potent nature. After further transmutation these particles or units gain the freedom of the ethers, and can fly from star to star, coming under the government of the solar system instead of under that of one small solid object.

In human affairs an analogy can be made. The human unit is first restricted to the limited nucleus of his family; later he is released into the larger sphere of his tribe; later he gains greater freedom, scope and possessions as a member of his nation. This is transmutation in human living. With each change he escapes into a broader living, he is stepped up into thoughts, habits, ideals and outlook of higher vibration. From the utter separatism of cave life, to the lesser separatism of tribe life, he has passed into the broader but still restricted phase of nationalism. He now stands upon the threshold of internationalism. This will be the greatest transmutation of all. At its inception he will become partly released from the nucleus of the nation, and strive to be a world citizen, living the fourth-dimensional life, and reaching ever forward for the plan, purpose and pattern which will bring him Utopia, a world set in order, and a universe whose riddles have been read.

The Dying Era of Separatism

It is not to be wondered at that little human beings are so self-important. In truth, they are so complex, there are so many sides to them, so many possibilities, and they are linked with so much that is happening all over the universe, that even throughout their blindest ignorance they seem to sense their potential significance. They sense it subconsciously, and they translate this feeling each man according to his wit or his wisdom.

We have understood that progress is brought about by a continuous cycle of the life force from the subtlest to the most solid matter and back again. This precipitation of the inner will and plan into visible matter we might call EXTERNALISATION. We can now study the way in which man himself, like a minute replica, repeats this universal process, having closely carried out this law of externalisation throughout the centuries of his development.

Man contains the essences of mineral, vegetable and animal life within his organism. He contains within himself the patterns, designs and qualities of all these kingdoms also. The lowest cells, microbes and crystal forms find place with the highest animal types from the time that he is in embryo throughout his gradual development. Man contains within himself an expression of everything, great and small, within the universe. He is subconsciously aware of this. He has, throughout his history, externalised into objectivity or physical manifestation, one by one, all those things which he embraces within himself. He has externalised mineral, crystal and plant forms in his architecture and sculpture. He has externalised his animal propensities in the form of animal deities. He has expressed his emotional and imaginative make-up in picture, in tapestry and in poem. He has externalised every muscle and sinew in his body in the form of tools, machines and engines. He has externalised his eyesight in the form of camera and cinema, his hearing in the form of music, telephone and wireless. At present he is endeavouring to capture in externalised instruments the very cosmic rays and forces which play through him. His achievements are incessant, untiring and astonishing.

Throughout it all he still remains unaware of the process to which he is contributing. He does not yet realise that he can only make and express in outward physical form those things which already exist within his own being. Every quality, activity, mechanism and force which he has so cleverly expressed in terms of machinery, chemistry and tool exists in all its aspects, latent or functioning, within the periphery of his own body, together with those other inventions and activities which will play their part in the future.

Because of the process of evolution man is bound to externalise every capacity, to mould and wield solid matter exterior to himself and make it express himself, as it were. What will happen when he has completed this process?

With this question our survey is being brought up to the point where we are to project our meditation into the future and visualise a new civilisation.

Let us make a solid foundation for our experiment by getting this process of externalisation quite clearly defined in our minds.

Man is filling the world with complicated machinery the while he has been neglecting himself. Humanity has become reduced to a condition of C3 health, C3 morals and C3 intelligence through pure neglect of and ignorance of its own inherent powers and its own potential perfection. There have been periods in history, such as the era of Greek culture, when this was not so, when man himself, with all his possibilities, was the object of study and development. The Greeks stressed man's physical perfection, whereas other ancient schools of thought usually stressed man's mental, psychic and spiritual powers. But the implication that the human being was a creature of stupendous potentialities was always to the fore. The gradual sinking of men's interests into purely objective and utilitarian aims, which have come to usurp all the foreground of his consciousness, has temporarily reduced life to a process of mental, moral and physical suicide. People have come to consider that they are on this earth to be comfortable and to be amused. They seek these states entirely outside of their own capacities, mostly in ways detrimental to everything they should be wishing to preserve.

For this reason they miss the true point and trend of human progressive activities.

Let us, however, follow the stages by which man copied the cyclic law and gradually crystallised everything within himself into outward external physical manifestation.

Primitive man was apparently well aware of his inherent powers. He responded to many more vibrations, or at any rate other vibrations than those to which most of us react now. He was naturally and involuntarily 'psychic' and telepathic and intuitive. The worlds of the inner dimensions held a paramount place in his life. He was intimately aware of those forces, which he called nature spirits, deities and devils. He could read and reproduce many of the symbols, patterns and shapes which have their origin in that stratum of the atmosphere which we have named the fifth dimension.

If we wish to put all the doctrines of primitive man down to 'imagination' we must first explain why his symbols, deities, colours and numbers bore the same meaning and significance all over the world at a time when intercommunication between continents was impossible. We must also explain why much of primitive men's beliefs are now being confirmed by modern science. We must also explain why, when later great civilisations arose, the most illumined minds directing those civilisations, such as Pythagoras, the Buddha, and even Christ Himself, concurred with many of these beliefs and gave them importance. All these great minds have declared man to be possessed of 'superhuman' powers which it is his duty to develop, and by means of which he learns to know and to control the hidden powers and entities and individualities of the invisible dimensions.

'All these things that I do and more, shall ye do!' said the Christ. He referred to the Seven Gifts of the Holy Ghost. These were the gifts which all men who develop themselves through living in accordance with cosmic or 'divine' law may hope to acquire. One of the foremost of these gifts was that of prophecy. Another was the power to interpret dreams and symbols. Two more were the power of healing, and the power to work 'miracles'. Clairvoyance was numbered among the seven, as was also the 'gift of tongues' or the power to be understood by persons of all nationalities. Perhaps the greatest of the gifts was that of wisdom. In the Bible the significance of the difference between wisdom, understanding and knowledge was carefully stressed. So also was the knowledge and thought which dwells in the *heart* differentiated from that which informs the brain. Now, after two thousand years of development, can we readily understand all these distinctions? How many good Christians, Buddhists or those of other faiths are deliberately working for the acquirement of those faculties held up to them by the great Teachers as their birthright? Most of the leaders of the churches would retire in confusion before such a question, and the mass of the public do not give it a thought. Yet we are told that such is the goal and purpose of our existence.

Man appears to have shelved his inner life while he gives his attention to the conquest of matter. He has left the understanding of himself and his own faculties to communities such as the spiritualists, who for more than fifty years have been demonstrating the existence of most of these 'superhuman' gifts. They and others have established the genuineness of clairvoyance, of prophecy, of healing, of phenomena in the realm of miracles and of extraordinary knowledge possessed by the sub- or super-conscious mind. Together with the hypnotists and the mesmerists they have done a valuable work in uncovering latent human powers, especially the capacity of the human mind to function in and as a part of the fourth dimension. The significance of much of this work has not yet been grasped by the public, perhaps not even by the experimenters themselves.

Meanwhile, men in the mass continue with their work of externalisation. With amazing cleverness they have produced television, by means of which it is possible to see things happening at a great distance. There have been numerous attested cases of people who, while under hypnotic direction, were able to project their sight to a distant town and correctly describe what was taking place there. There have been numberless cases of involuntary personal television whereby a person has been made aware of the dangerous predicament of a dear one, or of some other occurrence perhaps not relative to themselves. The fact that there exists within the human make-up something which corresponds to a television set has been proved beyond dispute. Yet up to date man neglects his own private ready-to-hand television set and goes to superhuman effort and trouble to manufacture artificial ones.

It is the same with wireless. Medical cases have been known where a person apparently contains a wireless receiving-set within his head, and involuntarily hears music from all quarters of the globe. The lunatic asylums are full of unfortunate people in whom the propensity to hear a variety of voices and sounds beyond the average, and in spite of themselves, is their only irregularity. The ancient savant, priest or mystic was usually instructed by voices unheard by men of less sensitive mould. Throughout the centuries it has been known that this personal wireless does exist. It has now been exteriorised into the wireless instrument that all may use without any personal effort or understanding of its laws.

It is the same case with the telephone. This takes the place of the capacity for telepathy which is one of the dormant faculties that man shares with many of the insects and animals, and which is still present to a marked degree in some of the remnants of earliest peoples.

The power to respond in various ways to the radiations of the fourth dimension is an inherent faculty belonging to the animal nature of man, which he shares with all the lower kingdoms. Animals, birds, fishes and insects, as well as the vegetable kingdom, all rely on 'instincts' which are governed by their intensive reactions to electrical and cosmic radiations. It has been realised that the antennae of insects, the feathers of birds, the tails of animals, and the hair of men and of plants are all intricate wireless receivers, or lightning conductors, which are used, when not in a state of atrophy, to bring a world of information to their owners. The unnatural and destructive influences of man's present mode of life have inhibited most of his 'wireless' faculties, and those which may still obtain are mostly involuntary, disorganised and distorted. Any person who therefore evinces potentialities or tendencies of these kinds is usually marked down as a pathological case, or at least as eccentric. In order to discover the existence of some of these cases the first places in which to look are in medical records or in lunatic asylums.

Human beings are indeed in a very sorry state compared with what they might and should be. This is due to the fact that for so long a period man has sacrificed himself utterly to the conquest of exterior physical matter. Physical matter has wielded a greater attraction for him than his own wonderful self, and he has automatically applied all his inspiration, his strength and his time to controlling and wielding it. Instead of mysticism, occultism or spiritualism, man has been governed by 'matter-ism' or materialism. He has concentrated upon the outer shell, the *least* powerful of the suggested seven dimensions. Therefore he is only about one-seventh as powerful a creature as he should be. Glance at the tired, dull, misshapen faces of a city crowd and this truth will come home vividly to us.

So far human beings have filled their lives with a tremendous accumulation of complications, machinery, factory, workhouse and shop, of a type which entails the youth of today toiling at automatic thought-destroying jobs before he has had time to profit by such education as is available. This is all done in ignorance that it is unnecessary, and that mankind could himself be trained to flower forth as the perfect instrument, enabled with his own mind to master the vibrations and control them at his will, using the human body as his one universal instrument.

We may suspect that a day may soon arrive when man achieves the development of all his own latent powers, and then factory, machine, instrument, mine and quarry will gradually be reduced, as largely the relics of a barbarous past.

This sounds like a fairy-tale, but it is the first hint of our approaching exploration into the future. Further meditations will lay the picture bare before us. We shall behold the time when the era of EXTERNALISATION is over, and men will reabsorb a large number of their inventions back into themselves where they truly exist.

A further phase of transmutation will have taken place. The forms embodied in machinery will have been raised to a higher vibration, a subtler dimension, the fifth dimension of mind-force, at last fully under the control of the innermost dimension of all, at which we may only hint at this time.

We have now finished the first part of our exploration. We have considered the way in which man has been outwardly developing and evolving, throughout history and at the present day. We have sought and found clues and explanations of this development in the underlying causes of scientific progress, and in the uncovering one by one of the laws of nature. We have seen how these laws of nature, as they were uncovered and brought into use, produced a steady march of ever-changing living conditions. We have deciphered the message of these changes, and understood in what manner humanity has failed to react to them, and to move along their unwaiting tides. We have grasped what a tremendous pull there is between the forward march of progress and the conservatism of short-sighted man, shackled by his habits and traditions and ruts.

We have realised that we are living at a tremendous moment in history, when a great era which has lasted thousands of years is dying, and a mysterious new era is coming to birth. What a time to be alive! We are caught and torn by both death-throes and birth-throes, in which vital forces are involved, that tear at our very heart-strings. The convulsions of these great forces have stirred humanity to the depths, swirling the dregs and the scum to the surface to temporarily confuse the issue with nobler elements already in action. The result bewilders us and we cannot discern the meaning of it all. Is humanity retrogressing? we ask.

So the battle continues between those who cling angrily to all that belongs to the dying period, and those who are ready to loose their hold on dead and crystallised ideas and gain a grander birthright in their place. These people are mixed, and fighting not always *vis-à-vis,* but side by side.

The great and wonderful dying era has nursed the development of the ego in man, involving self-assertion, creativeness in physical matter, the clinging to personal and national individuality.

The still greater and more wonderful dawning era will produce an utterly new consciousness in humanity, so different as to be hardly understandable, the consciousness of fusion with all things, so that little personal individuality seems no longer important or desirable, and man can truly say, 'I *am* all!' This change of consciousness will take many thousands of years to ripen, and will be fostered by amazing scientific discoveries changing entirely the habits of living and thinking.

The finger of science points implacably and irrevocably on towards this rapid fusion of humanity, and gives the decree that in living men shall radiate one to another without any veiling of their personality masks, thus bringing into full physical manifestation the fourth-dimensional world. For the law is that *everything unseen must become seen,* and must then be transmuted back again to its own realm, having gained strength in battle with physical vibrations. Man's personality, his emotional nature, has been waging its long war with physical life and wielded it most wonderfully to express his ardour and his devotion. The time for mental growth is now at hand. He is to learn to wield physical energies with his mind, in ways that he cannot now understand at all, but which will bring him to an undreamt-of power, and to a far less limited existence.

It is this entrancing world of future wonder which we are now ready to explore, in all its aspects. To do so we must ourselves in a small way wield and direct our minds into that realm which is to be their future heritage.

PART III

Contemplation—The Oracle Speaks

12

The Dawning Era of Change

The dawn of a new era! How thrilling that sounds! Has it ever happened before in this way? Is it one of those things like the 'modernity of the younger generation' which have always been in people's minds?

No. History has seen the dawn of many great civilisations who perhaps considered themselves all-important in the world —in some cases being unaware of the very existence of much of that world! Whereas the era dawning today embraces all the world, and is working already upon the minds of men everywhere, irrespective of nationality, religion and government.

The mind of Deity is meeting the mind of man through his interest in science and the laws of being. The crystal-clear and crystal-cold truths of Deity's planning, and the movement of His Will are becoming dimly discernible. They are absorbed by the subconscious of the scientific mind long before the brain can formulate them. The struggle of Einstein to express his Fourth Dimension resembled the urge of a man partially blind to explain colour to his totally blind companions. Einstein had glimpsed something, glimpsed it to the degree that he could only express it in figures and in the language of science. He had become aware that time and space do not really exist as we know them—that they are but little aggregations around ourselves, and that their reality in grander and greater terms must be something unrecognisable to us. He tried to express, in figures, and in the hard terms of this mechanical age, the mystery which has been embodied in symbol, in poem and in philosophy, in ancient Peru, Egypt, China, Tibet and India, by the Einsteins of the mystics' age.

For in fact we may rightly say that the mighty dying era has been the era of the heart, of the mystic and of the devotee, while the dawning era is that of the mind, the occultist, the one who deliberately co-operates with the plan of being.

'Be ye wise as serpents and harmless as doves,' commanded Christ, Whose mind was as profound as His heart was great. Two thousand years have passed before this admonition has penetrated into governing diplomacy. It is possible that Mr. Neville Chamberlain may go down in history as the first statesman to bring this spirit with definiteness to the forefront of politics, even though it turned out to have been premature. And be it remembered that he had the greater part of his public with him.

The old martial spirit which was a natural part of man's equipment is soon to die with a dying age—is actually dying in such countries as France, Britain and America already. These countries will do what they feel they have to do in martial respects, but the lust for battle has gone. It has gone in many other quarters too, although this is not yet so obvious.

Man's most primitive instinct, violence and antagonism, is losing ground rapidly. It has made havoc of his culture for aeons, but the glorious day of his delivery from this slavery is drawing near. This seems a strange thing to say at this time of unprecedented slaughter and persecution, but the very outcry against it all may give us a clue. Just as the drunkard plunges into his worst orgy on the eve of his regeneration, so also an aroused humanity behaves; the scum boils to the surface in the heat of blind struggles and strivings for a better world. For most men are idealists now! Whether they are Fascists, Communists, Democrats—they are all willing to suffer for their cause. This uprush of responsibility in their collective subconscious produces very often, as in the individual, first of all an orgy of the worst passions in their last attempt at mastery.

Let us remember this when we read of atrocities and outrages. We put an individual case in an institution or try to help him to reclaim himself, and are prepared to forget all if he does. The same rule must apply to the national unit.

The dawning age will be marked by a growing disinclination for recrimination, for sensationalism, for revenge and even for punishment. People will be too busy with reconstruction to spend time about that which is done. They will be too occupied in showing forth men's newly discovered possibilities to be sunk in inhibitions. These possibilities will negate the attraction of physical possessions to a large degree. It is not difficult to imagine what a difference this would make. In contemplation we are now drawing to us a vivid picture of the man of the future, an individual of quite different standards, ambitions, values and capacities to any we could find on the earth at present.

For it is necessary to realise that things are bound to come which will be far more wonderful than anything which has happened before. Progress and change has always gone on, but latterly it has become speeded up and intensified and world-embracing. It will lead rapidly to profound changes not only in man's outward living conditions, but in man himself.

If we could take a man who lived aeons ago at the beginning of the great passing era, and put him down in the middle of civilised life today, he would decide not only that the world was full of miracles and supernatural contrivances, but that modern man himself is a miraculous and supernormal being. He would be confounded, not so much by the crazy speed at which everything was moving and being done, but at men's power to support such speed and think in accordance with it. To our prehistoric friend the speed of train and car and 'plane would seem annihilating enough to a human being: even as confounding as being shot to the moon, walking on its surface, and being shot back, may seem to us.

Our reincarnated savage would look round on a populace who, in spite of an unhealthy, stunted and weedy appearance, were yet able to perform feats which necessitated a nervous system quite incomprehensible to him. The fact that everyone can perform without thinking the extraordinary act of reading; the possibility of any little girl of the people becoming a telephone operator! The daily life of the average business man, who steps from a terrifyingly speeding car into a train, then rushes into the bowels of the earth to the Underground, then up again, then into a rumbling motor-bus, then is swirled up in a lift to his office, and all this before he even begins his daily task!—then his rapid dealings with telephones, dictaphone, cables and calculations; and finally a repetition of the morning's madness before he finds himself once more approaching his own home and family!—such a daily achievement on the part of thousands of men and women would seem to the savage to show a race of beings who, although quite crazy, yet possessed superhuman and miraculous powers to an astounding degree, and an abnormal strength in order to stand it at all.

Future changes will bring even greater adjustments for man to make both in his activities and in himself, as we have visioned. Therefore, as we look into the far future, we shall find ourselves in the position of the savage! A new epoch will have ripened, which will have caused men's focus of living to shift from one dimensional realm into another, bringing into play different capacities in his make-up altogether. Our only plan will be to work gradually forward in our mental exploration, and consider the near future first of all.

For some time now people have been subjected to a new factor in life, that of vibration and radiation artificially produced and reproduced. This army of vibrations impinges upon human beings in their methods of transport, in factory machinery, in medical treatments, in the telephone and in the radio. This all produces a vast new impact on the physical and nervous systems. We know that a certain note can smash a wine-glass, and that many things will crack under a given vibration, whether applied as sound or in other ways.

What will be the eventual result of the bath of artificially produced vibrations in which humanity is coming more and more to live? The immediate results can be ascertained in a small measure by visiting nursing homes and asylums and consulting the case-books of our nerve-specialists. But this is only the beginning. A few generations will obviously have developed new characteristics altogether. What will they be?

Mankind is moving irresistibly towards fusion, both consciously and subconsciously. How will it come about?

The impossible has already happened, for even in political circles there are talks and plans around the ideal of 'Federation', these ideas having now got as far as the public lecture hall. Some talk of the Federation of a few countries, others of the Federated States of Europe, still others of a World Federation.

Thus we see that in spite of the terrible cruelties and atrocities and aggressions of which we hear, a new spirit is already alive, even in countries famed for their martiality and hot temper, a spirit which is willing to forget all and arbitrate for tolerant and impartial treatment, and co-operation and collaboration all round, just as soon as any or every nation shows readiness to subscribe to it.

In religious circles also we can see the same new spirit shining ever more brightly. Fellowships, congresses, societies struggle into existence, with the object of breaking down barriers and antagonisms between faiths, and drawing them together in a friendship and harmony undreamt of before our times.

Education also has its pioneers, while in science and medicine discoveries and inventions crowd each other so intensively that the public remain unaware of half of them, and the inventors stand awestruck before the possibilities opening up before them.

It is indeed a wonderful time in which to be alive—for those who *are* alive to it all!

So many changes are so close upon us. We will soon see the beginning of a definite and courageous attempt of a representative portion of humanity to make a stand against old habits and mistakes, and to begin actually and deliberately to lay the foundations for a new civilisation. This will not be the work of the 'recluse' or 'visionary', but of those at the helm of public affairs.

These things must and will come to pass. Not only do they represent the only way out, but humanity is too brave and too full of inspiration and endeavour to continue the process of self-destruction and self-immolation which threatens to end in international suicide.

It will be our endeavour to contemplate on the course which world salvage will take as the new age gathers strength and develops more obviously. We will consider our subject from the angle of politics, health, religion, science and living conditions. Working from the universal to the particular, we will begin with international politics, and coming changes in governing methods.

13

The Future of Government

The moment has now arrived for our projection into the future. We are not about to launch out into the unknown, however, which would have been the case had we waived the work of the preceding chapters.

As it is, we have already discovered a track, the track of evolution. We have mapped out its passage and its direction. We therefore are familiar with the broad aspects of the highway before us, and the goal to which it is tending. We have now to visualise the manner in which humanity will either press forward on that path, follow reluctantly, or be beaten along it. Assuredly there will be those of all three fashions. If we have placed our fingers discerningly upon the deepest pulse-beats of humanity we should be able to estimate their several strengths. Having thus a clue to the chord which the combined vibrations of the human family are sounding at present we should be able correctly to tune in to that which we wish to know.

It is just here that the scientific factor in Meditation takes its place. Scientists working with rays and vibrations are more and more proving the case for the theory of Meditation. The particular law in question is merely that of attraction between similar vibrations. Such vibrations are drawn to each other from anywhere in the universe, with the rapidity consequent on their fourth-dimensional quality.

If a thought of any particular subject is held sufficiently

strongly and one-pointedly, it takes on the inherent vibration of that subject, and therefore links with it and with all that pertains to it. As we first stated, so long as the mind sounds that vibration quite steadily, all knowledge connected with the subject of that vibration will flow into it. This, a purely scientific natural law, is the root cause of all inspiration. Ardency and longing, or other impulses, cause temporary one-pointedness of mind, and revelation comes.

'If thine eye be single thine whole body will be full of light.'

The subtle, delicate, but powerful process of contemplation we will now use to visualise the future; it is the basis for our assertion that it is *possible* for us correctly to see ahead.

We stated that our first subject would be the coming changes in human government.

The present period of wars and conflicts everywhere will have shaken up humanity from some of its deepest ruts. It will have lost confidence in existing forms of government, and long most passionately for some strong superior influence which will ensure future peace and safety. Many intellectuals who have long been wrestling with the problem of partially eliminating the sovereignty of states will put their findings before an interested public, who will be readier to accept them than might be expected. On all sides the tide of opinion in favour of Federation or World Unity will steadily rise. Efforts will be made to strengthen the position of the United Nations, but it will soon be understood that the invaluable part which that body can play will only be possible under the protection of an amalgamation of the governing power of all concerned.

For a long time World Conferences will thrash out the possibilities of a World Organisation and Federation. They will have to decide which are the national and which the international issues for control. They will be able to draw upon the experiment, experience and successes of the United States, of the United Kingdom, of Switzerland, of the U.S.S.R., and others for various factors in the process of international fusion.

After tremendous difficulties a start will be made. Possibly three or four countries will attempt the initial effort. The

Comm Market has already made a beginning in ways which would have seemed laughably impossible a few years ago.

While those of the broadest vision fight on for a World Organisation lesser beginnings and experiments will be attempted in many quarters.

As soon as nations have had the pluck to plunge into the federated system, various of its immediate results will become obvious.

The differences of currencies between the countries concerned will be equalised, and in time the same money will be used throughout. Tariffs and customs will of course be abolished, and the frontiers of countries will have lost a large part of their importance. National pride will not disappear. On the contrary each country will try to give the finest example of the ideal federated nation, and make the best possible contribution to the new era of civilisation. People will begin to hope. Confidence in a future never before deemed possible will give everyone a growing zest for life.

In a while the new amalgamation of nations will have become large and strong enough for all fear of war with other nations to be dismissed. Then gradually the fact that the menace of war is at last over will seep into the consciousness of the people, and life will take on a new colour altogether. The colossal sums hitherto spent on armaments will be freed for other uses, as well as the labour employed in armament factories, together with all the personnel and paraphernalia used in the customs, tariffs and other obsolete concerns of the kind.

There will be nothing else to do with these enormous assets except firmly to build up the new World Organisation and enter into a term of thorough social reconstruction. There will be more than enough of the money needed to rebuild every slum, and make a pride of every town and hamlet when the phase of expenditure on scientific prowess takes second place to humane and moral renaissance.

Without restrictions, food in abundance will flow in all

directions. A central world committee will so organise agricultural co-ordination that the grower of food will be henceforward the least-to-be-pitied mortal instead of, as now, perhaps the most.

In view of the resources accumulating in government coffers people with revolutionary ideas about the distribution of money will gain a hearing. Sooner or later one country will try out a new system altogether, in which every citizen is subsidised by the state from the time of birth, and entitled henceforth to the bare necessities of life. It may be found more convenient to work this system without money, using instead ration cards for rent, food, clothing and medical supervision, and education.

In the country where this system is first tried out certain results will soon become evident. A generation brought up without fear and dread of the future, and with an assurance of the necessities of life, will show an amazing improvement in health, and a growing reserve of vitality and energy. This will enjoy its natural outlet as initiative and creativeness. People will hardly know at first what to do with this vital personal energy. They will soon become incapable of sitting still to be spoon-fed with entertainment, and with the spectacle of other people doing things, as in sport, television, etc., they will all of them want to be expressing themselves. New psychological problems of this character will have to be tackled by the government. People will clamour to learn and to know and to do. Their artistic senses will come to life, arousing a love of nature, of handicraft, and of their own possibilities for beauty, in physique and in living.

Hospitals and asylums will empty, as colleges, farms and model towns fill up. Coming inventions will also do their share to change living conditions considerably.

When other countries see that with the system of subsidising the individual he becomes worth infinitely more to the state, which also halves its expenses in hospital treatment and so forth, all haste will be made to copy the new example. It will be found that the increasing vitality produces many pioneer spirits anxious to emigrate and to found new model communities. There will be a tremendous shifting of populations into some of the now almost barren areas of the Commonwealth.

It may be thought that the improvement in conditions will send up the birthrate to staggering proportions. On the contrary, a quite other situation will arise. To begin with, the fact that for the first time people's creative and artistic instincts are being thoroughly aroused and given full scope and appreciation will tend to make them lead naturally far more continent lives. Sexual satisfaction will no longer be one of the few comforts of the poor, nor the resource of the unfulfilled lives of the rich. There will no longer be the need to breed plentifully for cannon fodder, nor for factory fodder! The old-time capitalist employer will not exist under the new system. Furthermore, parents will not desire large families in the hope of being supported by them when they arrive at earning age. People will be taught and encouraged to have children only for love of them and pride in their upbringing. Subsidised children will do away with much of parental possessiveness and tyranny, and many one-time 'inhibitions' will cease to trouble them.

So far we have not touched upon future religious, educational or medical advantages at all, or even scientific ones. The Utopia we have visioned will come about to the degree we have stated through international governmental changes alone —purely through the ceding of sovereign state authority. It will be the result of the first major effort at integration, the casting down of the primitive elemental barriers of national rivalry, self-seeking and brigandage.

It goes without saying that such changes cannot come about except under the influence of the highest ideals, the most spiritual confidence, and the most practical of mentalities. They must be the result of true religion and true education. They will work, not as a vicious circle, but as a 'virtuous circle', the one achievement opening naturally out into another. We must realise also that this Utopia will be won only at the cost of superhuman effort, first among the few, and lastly among the people as a whole, when they have been taught to understand the goal in view. There will be, of course, many difficulties along the way, many passages of despair, many deadlocks, and even retrogressions. But the vision has already been seen and grasped by earnest minds in many lands. It will call irresistibly, and men will know no rest until they have brought it to fruition.

All those who say that it cannot be, that it must not be, and who fear, dread or deny the possibility of such changes, are merely people still chained to the third-dimensional vibration and all its thought accessories. Those to whom the vision appeals, who have faith in its goodness, and in its inevitability, are the people who are already drawn into the fourth-dimensional vibration of living and have given it their allegiance. Those who, while agreeing that such a Utopia would be marvellous, yet declare that human nature will not change, and that it is merely a dream, are existing with a foot in either dimension, and will be very nerve-racked people ! Finally there are those who not only believe in the coming Utopian state, but are energetically planning it in detail. These happy forerunners have already touched with their courageous minds the vibrations of the fifth dimension of living, and are humanity's greatest benefactors.

They will soon be busy with much novel work. National and International Psychology will constitute one of the new sciences. The development of the ideal of Federation will cause the conception of a 'family of nations' to grow, until each nation takes on in people's minds the aspect of one member of a family and comes to be regarded as an individual. The psychologising of the individual person will be developed to a most interesting degree. The same technique will be applied to the nation-as-an-individual.

The especial vocation of each human being will become a growing study, involving an understanding of his particular potential contribution to society, together with the especial virtue which in his case makes it possible, and its complementary vice. In the same way it will come to be recognised which is the particular part any nation is to play, and which should be her unique contribution to the whole human family of nations. Her especial virtue will be acknowledged and she will be put on guard against its complementary vice. In this way each nation, with its unique gift to offer to the community, will acquire its own importance and individuality and the appreciation and aid of the entire world—to a far greater degree than any autocratic sovereign state has ever been able to command.

In such ways the lesson will gradually be learned that it is only by eliminating those barriers which were especially erected to preserve individuality, importance, possessions and power, that these attributes can really be attained. It is only when an individual clings to *nothing* that he can gain everything. 'He who loses his life shall gain it.' An entity, whether a person or a nation, gains so much extra power, vitality and interest, the moment fears, inhibitions and restrictions are cast away, that his presence becomes a necessity to those around him. He need never fear for his 'place in the sun'. He has become a sun himself, because he has thrown off all which impeded his natural radiations, and all will delight in his rays.

People have become blinded to these grand simple truths during the long reign of separatism. The manifold lessons which fourth-dimensional activities are bringing home to them will soon accustom them to think in terms of radiations, and then conceptions of life will inevitably change.

Students of national psychology will make it clear that nothing can ever destroy a nation, even a very small one. We see such nations still survive after having been invaded, annihilated, crushed under a foreign heel, and lost to sight for hundreds of years. They are liable to rise from their own ashes at any time, and show that their language, customs and characteristics have miraculously survived it all. The Jew gives us a classic example of the deathlessness of a racial entity, and many other different cases of survival will come to mind.

Therefore those who fear that Federation and fusion between states will cause them to disintegrate and degenerate might first study history. They might even study a small country like England, which began life in the usual way as a conglomeration of little warring states, but has been closely welded as a nation for around a thousand years. Yet her different counties, having existed all the while without the slightest barrier between them, with the populace free to move from place to place as they will, have still preserved their various characteristics, their customs and their accents—in some places to a remarkable degree, as, for example, the little Duchy of Cornwall, whose natives still speak of those from outside its borders as 'foreigners'.

The amalgamation of the nations which is to come will take place in some respects spectacularly, but also in subtle gradual ways, so that many of the most important modifications pass with hardly any notice. At times disturbance, friction and conflict will appear to outweigh the progress which is being made. But the pioneers will never quite despair. Their inspiration will be fed by the secret drive of evolutionary forces beneath the surface, and in spite of itself, long-suffering humanity will at last become aware that in truth a better civilisation has been born than they had ever dreamed of.

14

The Future of Faith

We are each the result of what we believe. The muddles in the world today testify to muddled beliefs, and therefore to muddled motives. Men have muddled the issues and the clear-cut instructions of the fine religious doctrines which have been bequeathed to them. They have superimposed their own separatist attitude upon them, and flying straight in the face of implicit statements and commands, have rearranged them into a compromise with their preferred way of living.

Christ instructed those who would preach His gospel to go forth without money or possessions, living the simple life. Man has replied with such a construction as the opulent Church of Rome! So many and so flagrant are the ways in which men have disobeyed the decrees of their faiths that we need not waste time with a description of them. We are now looking to the future, the past is sufficiently known to us.

We have seen that so far men have been largely ruled by their emotions, especially in regard to their religion. In fact a man's religion has been definitely confined to the realm of the emotions. For him to have considered his religion to be on a par with scientific thought and practical common sense would, for some peculiar reason, have been looked upon as blasphemous! This is because the spiritual life of man has been strictly treated as something intangible, psychic, vague, mystic, ecstatic—the cause of this, as we have seen, lying in the fact that he has been passing through the era of the mystic, the era ruled by emotion.

The new mental era will bring in quite different conditions relative to men's spiritual life. The same undercurrent which stimulates them to fusion and federation in world politics will influence them in religious affairs. This influence is obviously, of course, already in action. The seeds have germinated, producing several movements such as the World Fellowship of Faiths and the Inter-religious Fellowship, which have been growing and developing for some years. It is uphill work. All those who dislike change declare that a world-religion is impossible, that a person's spiritual life is a personal thing which cannot be regimented, and so on. The fact that so far a narrow regimentation is just what has been practised in many communities escapes these critics !

A World Religion will come, and will in time be considered the only sane, normal and natural condition. Men will look back upon the times when bloodshed, bigotry, irrationality and corruption sheltered safely under the wing of religion with incredulity. If federation of the nations can come about without damage to a person's national patriotism and individuality, as we have foreseen, then a federation of religions can develop also without destroying the personal approach to divinity, but, rather, enhancing it.

People considering themselves Christians at once protest, with the usual separative partisanship which they believe to be loyalty, that Christianity is *the* faith and Christ is *the* Saviour, and nothing else should be considered. They forget that true Christianity has never yet been practised, and no one has therefore had the chance to appreciate its value or its beauty. If once a sufficiently large community were to live truly as Christians they might draw every other faith under their banner purely through the wonderful results of their so living. But until Christians *are* Christians they have really no right to talk of Christianity—it does not yet exist ! Christ and His Teachings exist, but Christianity as He desired it is yet to come. There have been glorious isolated cases of Christian lives, but a truly Christian Government, Christian Law Court, and Christian Church has never been established—so how, then, could the people follow? They have only been muddled. The Government of a so-called Christian country must at least bow to the Ten Commandments—one of which is simply 'Thou shalt not kill'. The Government send people out to war, the Church blesses them! The Law Court condemns a man for killing another—and kills him in its turn! The Church is against adultery and divorce, while the Law condones and arranges it. It is all ridiculous. As soon as the mental era begins to ripen people will see how ridiculous it is. Many of them see it already, and instead of revolting against *inadequate* legal and religious attitudes, they revolt against law and religion altogether. They are then called 'moderns', and people leave it at that. This paragraph will probably be called 'pacifist'— another name meaning nothing much. The question in point is not 'pacifism' but true Christianity, which is a vital question for everyone.

The Buddha preached the technique of BEING. The Christ added to this the technique of DOING. Right action is founded upon right being. The Doctrine of Christianity was, in a way, superimposed upon Buddhism, carrying the spiritual development of man a step further. It crowns all former religions, was brought by the greatest Teacher of them all, and is still far beyond men's powers of achievement. We have to realise that men are graded in many different categories, of many different rates of vibration. So long as this is the case there will be religions to suit them all. As soon as a man has developed to a certain stage he will recognise the true Christian religion as his goal, and embrace it. If he has been a good Buddhist he will learn to worship both Christ and Buddha, seeing Them in Their right relationships. The Easterner will learn that the Christ of the West appeared also in the East under another name. The more people bring their minds to bear upon the truths underlying the complexities of traditional religious doctrines, the more clearly they will perceive the same set of divine laws and teachings shining through them all.

The transition from the era of mystic emotional religion into the coming era of occult or mental religion will show forth Christ and His words in a different light. He will at last be understood as a profoundly scientific and practical Teacher, with a mind full of tender humour and logic. The true occultist will be the Christian *par excellence,* worshipping Christ, as they already do, as the 'Master of all the Masters, Head of the Hierarchy, Teacher alike of Angels and of men'.

It may be asked in despair : 'Why, then, is it taking so long for those who desire, generation after generation, to become good Christians, to approach anywhere near to their ideal?'

It would seem that a great religion is like a beacon shining from the unknown future, setting a goal ahead of humanity, pointing to the trend of its development. A great religious doctrine is in reality a prophecy of the destiny of man's soul. Science in its own divine secret language explains how that destiny will be attained.

Christ held up the fourth-dimensional way of living to a humanity still third-dimensionally oriented. He taught the art of living the radiatory life, the life without barriers, classes, prejudices, enviousness, or possessiveness. He even foretold the attainment of personal fourth-dimensional powers when He said those words to which we have already referred : 'All these things which I do and more shall ye do after me.' He preached a way of life which sounded madly impossible to the bulk of His hearers, and still seems sadly impossible to most of us today. However, there is a growing vanguard of people who not only deem such living possible, but are planning to put it into execution. Such movements as the World Fellowship of Faiths, 'Moral Rearmament', Federal Union, are inspired by the real Christian spirit of unity and collaboration, just as are the United Nations, and the many world congresses, international meetings and world fairs. They all show the growing desire for unfettered human relationships and harmonious co-operation.

True Christianity is on the way. The Church will break out of the shackles of the old era, in which she ruled by fear of consequences, and made of her doctrines a rather depressing, morbid, solemn and perfunctory programme. Spiritual life will become a thing of joy, indulged in for its own sake, bringing Heaven *now* instead of saving from Hell hereafter. This will entail very great changes in the outlook on spiritual matters. They will come to fuse with all other interests in life instead of being merely one phase of it, kept for Sundays. Spirit will be regarded as beauty and meaning in life, enriching every action and every object with worth. It will be understood that matter is just crystallised spirit and spirit is transmuted matter, and the purpose of this interplay will be ardently sought. This new approach to life will come about through the gradual fusion of 'religion', 'occultism' and 'science'. These three great facets of truth will become inseparable in men's minds, as they were before the Age of Separatism waxed strong. In the mental era the Mind of Deity will be studied and worshipped in the laboratories. The findings of the scientists will be given forth in the churches. For a long period people will almost forget the Love of God in their devotion to the Mind of God. This will stimulate their own minds and they will become eager to use them.

The craze for knowledge will eagerly invade the religious sphere. For the first time people will begin seriously to study their own religion, and ask a great many very awkward questions. Inconsistencies, mistranslations, and duplications in other fields will all be pounced upon in the light of energetic searching. Religions will have to be remodelled to suit growing public intelligence. People will seek for enlightenment among religions other than their own. All religions will have to be described in school curriculum. Occultism, mysticism and spiritualism will each come in for inquiry, and the barriers between them will be seen to be absurd. They will insensibly be bridged over. Science will soon find its natural place in this amalgamation, as will the place which music and the arts should play in man's spiritual and physical life. This will come about through people's growing sensitivity to and understanding of radiations. We shall learn of this when we consider the future in its relation to health and science.

Changing conditions in social living, in education, and in physical conditions, will bring about the development of certain latent human faculties. These will in time produce so much fusion of the various aspects of life in the human mind that men will cease to consider the existence of such a subject as 'religion' at all. They will have become aware through their heightened senses of the teeming world which lies just beneath the threshold of our five-sense consciousness of today. They will no longer need to 'believe' in a Creator or in the 'after life'. Their blossoming mentality will recognise certain laws, certain facts, and certain logical arrangements and trends in life around them. Their stimulated senses will discern the mighty Presence which breathes throughout the universe. The new conditions of living which we foretold in the last chapter having set free a great store of vitality, of brain power and of *joie-de-vivre* in human beings, they will sense divinity most vividly in Nature around them, in the beat of every bird's wing, in the tossing of sea waves, in the atom under the microscope, and in the brilliance of the scientist at work upon it, in the miracle of their own birth, nourishment and growth, and in the potentiality of their own minds. Life will become a constant tuning-in with Divinity.

If you were to ask a man of the far future 'What is religion?' he would look at you in surprise and answer, 'Why—everything!' The idea of a religion separated off from education or any other phase of life would appear to him absurd, unnatural and unpractical. The idea that a human being could be so pitiful, so blind and so mentally impoverished as to strive, after thousands of years of development, to prove survival through pathetic experiments with phenomena, will appear fantastic to the man of the future, who will have no need of any such assurance.

The developments towards this stage will take place gradually, their growth being contributed to by ever-changing conditions on all sides. The anxiety, pain and torment which a large portion of humanity will have passed through by the end of this period of warfare and conflict will have roused up the human spirit to a new sense of responsibility for the future of the race, and an earnest desire for truth, enlightenment and inspiration. A great wave of longing will go out to the Christ, whether as from Christians to their Founder, or from earnest individuals to the Spirit of Peace and Goodness Whose existence he senses. This wave of longing will grow ever stronger, transmuting men's vibrations to a finer and more sensitive key, until finally they synchronise with that which they seek, and a glorious revelation and illumination will break upon them.

This tremendous event will take place during the lives of those who are already born. We can look upon the little child of today with awe and envy because he will live to see the greatest event of the new era—the 'second coming of Christ'. This event is foretold and expected by many thousands of people to occur before the end of this century. Therefore it is not one of the 'original' thoughts coming to us in this book, but it finds its place in our vision nevertheless. People have, of course, little idea as to the form or manner in which this second coming will take place. But we can see that it will actually be the people themselves who journey to the 'Christ within' through having finally tuned up the vibrations of their consciousness to function strongly in the fourth dimension, the realm of radiation, of warmth and attraction, of love—the realm wherein Christ moves and links with us.

The collective suffering and stimulation which humanity is going through all over the world will result in a fourth-dimensional consciousness being brought to birth in numberless people in every land. While the Western Christian recognises his Christ, what of the East? The Easterners, who have still preserved to a certain extent their link with the fourth dimension, their assurance of, rather than belief in, Deity, their unquestioning acceptance of survival, and their acknowledgment of rebirth or reincarnation, will surely take easily to the further development ahead of them. In the East they believe in the Lord Maitreya, Who is to appear again amongst men. Occultists declare that this is the Eastern name for our Christ, and that when revelation breaks upon both the East and the West they will discover that their awaited Lords are one and the same Being. If this is the discovery ahead of mankind, then it can clearly be understood how easy the path will be made for the coming 'World Religion'. The coming mission of the Son of God, worshipped throughout so many civilisations under so many guises, will be the ultimate fusion of men's spiritual lives into a harmonious whole. How long it will be before this uniting is achieved, and how much of difficulty and conflict will have first to be passed through, need not concern us here. We have glimpsed the glorious vision of the future through the facet of what we call 'religion'. We must proceed to fill in our picture through the medium of other facets.

In this connection we may say that the underlying form upon which matter is built is that of the prism! When Deity passes through the prism of matter He appears to our eyes as divided into certain rays or qualities. One of these divisions, which we call Love, builds the fourth dimension, while another, which we call Intelligence, builds the fifth dimension. As we study the different aspects of human or divine activity we are only shifting our focus from ray to ray, or looking at Deity through another facet of the prism.

In this chapter we have touched upon the way of Love, the Son, Christ, the Founder of religions, the Dweller in the fourth dimension, the world of the heart.

We will now turn to contemplate the future of that other great aspect of Deity, shining through matter, the ray of Intelligence, with the manifold expressions of its creative energy, its pattern, plans and designs, and the realm it has built—the fifth dimension!

15

How Science Will Change the World

As we are entering an era in the history of mankind when the mind will reign supreme it follows that knowledge will be given first place in men's hearts. This so-called scientific age will eventually develop into a truly scientific age, wherein people seek to make a science of the whole of their lives instead of leaving the pursuit of exact knowledge to be a profession for the few. This attitude will have both its advantages and its disadvantages. There will be, as always, many dear enthusiasts who spoil and endanger everything through exaggeration. But the conviction that the scientific attitude to life ought always to be applied, just as the 'religious' aspect ought to be undifferentiated and all-pervading, will grow steadily under the increasing influence of the fourth dimension.

In this connection let us not forget the overlapping of evolutionary phases. While we were living the third-dimensional life we were preparing for the fourth dimension, firstly through discovering. As soon as we begin to live the fourth-dimensional life we shall prepare for the fifth-dimensional life, firstly by discovering it! We are now at the intermediate stage between these two, the time of the switch-over, which is why there is so much confusion.

As the various sciences, such as natural history, chemistry and electrical engineering draw nearer to the source of things they will insensibly draw nearer to each other. They will also inevitably approach closer to the religionists, the occultists and the artists. What will be the results of this rapprochement?

As the whole of scientific interest will be mostly involved with the subject of radiations, it will soon be realised that one of the most potent instruments of radiation is the human mind. As soon as many phenomena of the mind which are now sceptically waved aside are scientifically understood and accepted, an intensive period of mind study and mind culture will make its appearance. The possibility of prevision through carefully trained thought and meditation, similar to what we are now doing in this book, will be accepted. The enormous help which certain methods such as this might be to science will become apparent. People who are already trained in thought control and meditation will be eagerly sought out. They will be discovered in the ranks of those who go under the names of 'occultists', 'mystics' or, in rare cases, 'mediums', but whom we can class under the name of 'mind-scientists'. Soon these latter will work in close collaboration with orthodox scientists as well as with the advanced creative artists.

The result of this fusion will be interesting. The mind-scientist when using his powers of prevision will be able to indicate to both scientist and artist the trend of evolution, and the discoveries and events to anticipate. By this means the scientist of the future will already know what he is going to discover, he will know what to look for and expect, and he will be saved a vast amount of time and labour and lack of recognition. The artist also will be given inspiring visions for his works of art and will thus be enabled to give forth impelling messages to the public.

Scientists will be drawn together (for the same reason that the threads in a spider's web converge to a centre—their ultimate goal is identical) to uncover the forces and the secrets of the fifth dimension. Their approach to this is bound to be along the avenues of radiation, because it is the fourth dimension which links the third to the fifth. Men have only touched the fringe of the colossal world of radiations, a world in which our earth swings like a little pellet, influenced by the millions of rays of all kinds and sizes which play through it.[1] Each

[1] See *The Initiation of the World.*

time the scientist isolates, studies and uses a fresh radiation he opens up new possibilities, new discoveries and new inventions, any of which may have a profound effect upon the lives of his fellow-men.

The vista which stretches before us into the future shows the most amazing new world being rapidly opened up by the scientists, and an array of discoveries which changes life like a fairy-tale. Indeed, that is a good simile, because the coming age is nothing if it is not an age of Magic! We know that Magic is supposed to be a power that man wields in his own person, over forces which are behind physical manifestation.

The greatest of the coming changes will be in man himself.

In a world where radiations reign he will begin to use his own instrument for their control—the mind! The results of this will be almost beyond our present powers of understanding, so we must go slowly.

Where shall we begin in our enumeration of coming wonders? Many of them are not so much new inventions as further developments of existing ones. In photography, for instance, a more delicate lens and developing medium will be invented, with which strange and inexplicable pictures will be taken. By the time this invention is perfected it will be known that photographs are being obtained of 'non-solid' life, of innumerable strange phenomena all inextricably mixed, which are held in the ether. A vast amount of trouble and controversy will go on over these strange impressions, which will be claimed by spiritualists as their final proof. The scientists will insist that they are purely 'scientific'. At last a system will be perfected by means of which lenses are tuned to a variety of vibrations, and then the fact of the different ethers and their contents will become established.

All this while clairvoyance among ordinary people will develop rapidly and will be corroborated by these photographs. The art of psychometry, or the reading of the ethers, will take its place as a serious science. It will be learnt that certain strata of the ethers are impressed with images of places and events of the past, in the same way as would be a photographic film. As, however, these impressions are made on fourth-dimensional substance instead of third-dimensional (or physical), they are necessarily under different laws to those of the photographs we now know. They are under the laws of radiation, and may be of many classes and due to various causes. They may either belong principally to the class of simple images impressed upon the ether from physical forms, or they may be originated from the fifth dimension, rayed out from their source as we have already described, in which case they can be of any size.

It will be discovered that a certain combination of atmospheric conditions, of heat, moisture and electrical content, will enable the ordinary human eye, when just at the right angle, to catch glimpses of some of these etheric photographs. It will be realised that something of the kind has occurred every time a 'ghost' has been observed in the past. It will be learnt that when a person walks along, his image is lightly impressed upon the ether along the whole length of his passage. Attempts will be made to photograph this in the endeavour to obtain an etheric moving-picture! These attempts will eventually succeed. It will then be realised that a certain type of the well known phenomena of the ghost who walks at a given hour, even at a certain day of the year, can be scientifically explained, being due to definite atmospheric conditions, coupled also with astrological conditions, which cause certain impressions in the ether to become temporarily vitalised.

A very important fact will in this way come to light. This is that any disturbance or particular vibration which is set up in the ether at a certain spot persists there more or less indefinitely, according to its strength. This will explain the curses which the old Egyptian and other 'mind-scientists' were able to attach to tombs, statuettes, jewels and other articles. This same type of 'curse' can be impressed upon any part of house or land through an occurrence sufficiently forceful having taken place there.

Scientists, having got so far, will then inquire why it is that only certain persons and events are impressed upon the ether sufficiently clearly to produce a 'ghostly' record. After much research it will at length be ascertained that a lasting impression on the ether is formed under the electrical heat of strong emotion, which has usually been of a tragic nature, but need not necessarily be so.

Under the novelty of these discoveries many new occupations and hobbies will spring up. People will practise clairvoyance and also etheric photography. Finally, they will try to make impressions upon the ether themselves and photograph them. In this and other ways the earliest attempts at the Magic of the new age will have their inception. People will have begun so effectively to control their mind-power that they can, in a crude and elementary manner be it granted, wield etheric matter with it. The discovery and the practice of these capacities will, of course, take place under the stimulus of the craze for everything mental which we have already mentioned.

Some of the coming wonders of photography are already in course of experiment, such as those claimed by Dr. Ruth Drown. Apparently she is already able to obtain a photograph of any part of a person's anatomy if she places a drop of his blood in her apparatus, no matter how far away he may be. We have already discussed the way in which an image radiates out in all directions from its source. If it links with another portion of its originator which has become separated off, a circuit is made, so that there is a continuous flowing to and forth of that particular stream of life. It is like a living electric telephone-line along which many things can be caused to flow. Through causing certain vibrations to flow along it, Dr. Drown claims to effect healing. This is the beginning of a science which will broaden out into amazing channels. People will take with them a drop of the blood of relative or dear one in a scientific receptacle, and be able to speak to them and see them along its rays. Later, other methods will be discovered by means of which anyone anywhere can look upon any place he so desires. The instrument which we now know as television will have become obsolete.

Later on again, people will find it superfluous to carry about the little blood-receptacles of their friends. They will learn instead how to memorise the vibrational number of any person and impress it upon the ether to form their mutual receiving station. We have, indeed, travelled many, many generations into the future in order to see the attainment of such achievements, but as it is the long view which has been so much missing in average human thought, a little practice can only be good!

Let us withdraw our focus nearer to our own times and consider what are to be the next steps in scientific discovery. Many of these are close upon us. They will mostly be in' the sphere of electricity, the phenomenon which has already played such an enormous part in our lives, although no one can say definitely what it is. All we know is that a tremendous storage of power is flowing through life, and that its activities and manifestations have been classed loosely for everyday usage under the name of 'electricity'.

One day quite soon an entirely different kind of electricity will be discovered which will bring as many profound changes into human living as the first type did. This new electricity will move in a finer ether than does our familiar kind, and thus will be nearer in vibration to the fifth dimension, to the innermost source of things, that realm of the 'withinness' wherein all is held poised by a colossal force, that same force which is packed within the atom. Electricity number two will be unthinkably more powerful than our present electricity number one. At first it will be released at tremendous expense and risk, by methods closely connected with the present-day smashing of the atom. For a long time its danger will outweigh its usefulness. At last a comparatively easy and simple way of releasing it will be discovered, and its uses will come well under control. It will be so cheap and so powerful that the necessity for coal, petrol, oil and gas will quickly pass away. This will cause a great upheaval in labour conditions, releasing men from much unhealthy and unnatural drudgery.

The new electricity will not flow along wires. It will be controlled by the law of vibrations as wireless is. Houses will be tuned up to take it while being built. It will eventually be in use under something resembling thermostatic control, so that it automatically comes into action at dusk. The problem for the inventors will then be, not how to turn it on, but how to be able to turn it off!

Vehicles will be able to draw this electricity from the air as they go along. This will arouse profound speculation. In time the insatiable mind of future man, busy with his experiments of mind-control, will realise that this new electricity must be flowing through his own body just as every other radiation does. He will learn to store it and control it, through scientific breathing, and thus be enabled to regulate his own temperature and resist the cold to an astonishing degree, much as the Tibetan lamas have always done.

This may come to be very necessary, because the planet herself will be going through changes also, which, over the long periods of time we are visualising, will bring fundamental modifications. Human beings, singly and collectively, are raising their vibrational tempo under the stress of evolutionary processes, and are becoming transmuted, so that in company with all physical matter they are becoming hotter, more luminous and lighter in weight. This whole process collectively is bound up in our planet, whose total vibrationary rate is also steadily rising.

The earth is thus becoming lighter in weight and hotter. The earliest results of this are not far to seek. They begin with a shifting and a melting of the vast icefields near the North Pole. Scientists have already observed that this is taking place, and that the climate in the northern regions is definitely growing warmer. As these vast quantities of ice break up and flow out into the oceans they will bring, temporarily, terrible cold spells in a world because it is growing warmer! This cold will give great impetus to the development of heating power on a big scale from the new electricity. There will be so much money available because of improved international conditions that the new heating, lighting and power will be applied on a scale which will enormously change the lives of almost every-one.

Another of the most interesting of the developments of the near future will be in relation to people's attitude to animals. Various factors will be responsible for these developments. The cessation of antagonism, warfare and slaughter between men will, within a few generations, set free a deep and natural horror of killing any living creature. Also the intensive use of the mind in new ways will necessitate new forms of nourishment in which flesh-food will gradually cease to play any part. Uncooked seeds and flowers, for instance, will be found to contain many of the elements of nourishment which future man is going to require. There will also spring up a school of thought, the School of Distillation, which will distil the essences of many strange things for food.

In a comparatively short time the use of animal flesh for any purpose will be considered low barbarism. Later on, the new processes of ether photography will reveal amazing facts about animals hitherto quite ignored. The effect upon the ethers, and therefore upon the human psyche, of curtailing animal independence will be startlingly exposed. The evolutionary function of men in respect of the animal world will come dimly to be realised. Animals themselves will respond surprisingly to the new attitude taken towards them, as well as to the new living conditions of men. A peculiar rapprochement will take place, and, finally, men and animals will find a method of conversing together. This, my brothers, may sound fantastic, but it is really our total blindness and deafness at the present time to all but a very few vibrations which is fantastic!

The tremendous joy and fulfilment which animals will gain out of this future development will be vividly understood by all who love them. The intense, almost heartbreaking, efforts of the advanced animals of today to express their thoughts to us are easily recognised. It remains for us to devise a method of communication. This discovery will be the sensation of its current age. From their animal friends men will then learn certain things which have hitherto eluded them. In some communities men will even study with the animals. It will be realised that a true and complete man is the link between the spiritual kingdom and the animal and lower kingdoms in nature. A man must, therefore, be first of all the perfected animal, secondly the perfected human being, and thirdly the awakened son of God, the consciously spiritual entity. The function of humanity is to blend and correlate these three capacities.

When men truly realise this obligation and destiny they will turn with brotherhood and their full love and attention to the animals. They will endeavour to reacquire all those marvellous animal 'instincts' and powers which have long lapsed and atrophied within themselves. Not only will it be considered essential to develop a body as beautiful, rhythmic and healthful as those of the animals, but the etheric, or sensitive, side of animal living will be sought after too—their wonderful reactions to a variety of wavelengths, which help them in danger, in their search for food, in their sense of hearing and of scent, and in regulating mating and feeding. Men will practise these arts with the help of the animals themselves. The underlying inspiration of this is, of course, not new. It is many centuries since animals were kept by the priesthoods for intimate study; for instance, as an aid to the practice of yoga. Even at the present day one hears of interesting experiments taking place in Scandinavia, where it has been discovered that a stork will build her nest only at the place where certain vibrations meet in the air, which, apparently, give the necessary stimulation for the production of progeny. It seems that if a hitherto childless woman changes her bed to a position immediately below the stork's nest, and therefore within that fertilising vibration, that a child is often the result. This brings to light the origin, lost in the mists of antiquity, of the legend of the stork bringing children.

In the future that is coming, when intelligent communication is set up between man and animal, it can be imagined into what a surprising new world the latter will initiate him. This will be only one of the important innovations which will be introduced through men's growing intimacy, not only with the physical and chemical aspects of the fourth dimension, the world of radiation, but with the intelligent heart aspect, the radiations of understanding, of unity and of fusion with all things. For it will be love, the Christ-love, which will set men free to roam consciously in the radiatory world, penetrating on the rays of their own hearts into the myriad living types around them, with whom they will find that their true consciousness, escaped from the old shells and barriers, is so closely interlocked.

16

The Health of Our Descendants

As we consider a future in which all aspects of life are going to blend more and more, it is difficult to arrange our findings categorically, under separate headings such as health and science. There will be much overlapping. The whole question of health will come ultimately to be closely bound up with education, with psychological and with spiritual training, with an understanding of science in its relation to the human being, with the effects of colour, sound and perfume, and with many other factors, so that it will be impossible to determine the limits to the study of health.

At the present time, through separative treatment, health has reached the same impasse as economics and other human affairs. But we are already familiar with this subject,[1] and our viewpoint is now to the future. We have noted that health will be enormously improved through the effects of changing international relationships. A number of fears will be removed from men's consciousness, such as fear of war, of want, and of being not wanted. The change that this will bring after a few generations to the standard of health and of mental alertness and initiative will be so great that it is difficult to visualise it. People will no longer need to be *distracted* from all the worry of living by hectic entertainment and unnatural habits. Everyday life itself will become a continuous joy, to be relished with man's growing store of energy. This will make the consuming

See *The Initiation of the World.*

of stimulants such as alcohol, meat and tobacco nauseous and unnecessary to him.

The cultivation of health, beauty and knowledge will become a deep-seated craze. The tremendous part which the cosmic rays with their radiations and wavelengths will come to play in men's lives will gradually make them more and more ray-conscious. As new rays with their amazing powers[1] continually come to light, much will be understood of the secret influences on human health. The rays, which emanate from stellar bodies, and produce strong electrical and chemical influences according to their varying intersections, will be found to explain the secret underlying astrology. The astrology of the future will come into being.

As people grow more highly sensitive they will begin to feel and even to see some of these rays, and understand their own particular reactions to them. They will learn to regulate their lives in accordance with the help that ray influence can give them, just as do the animals; learning to respond, individually, to the best times, for them, for great mental effort, for periods of rest, for mating, for spiritual endeavour, and for many other activities. By these means much waste of effort, straining of nerves and many mistakes will be avoided, and creative inspiration will be the lot of increasing numbers of people.

The reason why night is meant for sleep will be another of the more important discoveries made. People will come to understand how the electric polarisation changes as day passes into night, and how they shorten their lives and undermine their health by keeping late hours and fighting against the tides of nature. Night life will come to be deprecated not only as suicidal, but as a sure way of degenerating mental capacity. To miss sleep will be known to be far more important than to miss food. People will cherish the tremendous feeding power of sleep. They will learn, also, of other strange and beneficial things which happen to them during slumber, which activities will come to acquire as much importance as the things which they do by day. They will become sensible to the

[1] See *The Initiation of the World*.

influences which play through them during all the twenty-four hours, and they will learn which parts of the day are more suitable to various of their activities.

All these growing awarenesses will do much to lift humanity out of the shocking conditions of bad health, shortened life span and impaired intellect which are so oppressively prevalent today that they are accepted as almost the normal and inevitable conditions.

Many present-day diseases will pass away, but others will take their place. These will mostly be diseases of sensitivity and of overstimulated mentality. Mankind will have overcome the grosser physical diseases, but will become prone to the attacks of 'mental microbes'. Men will have to battle with the strange and embarrassing afflictions which their growing response to subtle forces will entail until their organisms have had time to adjust themselves.

The influence of fourth-dimensional living upon the treatment of health will bring in many radical changes. It will be realised that a competent community should be able to prevent disease rather than have to cure it. As so much reorganisation will be going on in the world it will be quite natural for the medical system to come in for its share. In conjunction with the beginnings of World Government Control some kind of an international health control committee will be set up. In time the very obvious solution to the problem of human health supervision will be grasped in all its simplicity, and great innovations will be made, to the interest and delight of a public becoming determinedly health-conscious.

It will be realised how pathetically inadequate is the present-day system of the management of health and disease. The fact that a doctor has no right to examine his patient until he is sent for because of some obvious and advanced symptom, is ridiculous. Under existing arrangements often a doctor is only brought into contact with his patient when it is already too late to effect a cure, or at any rate a permanent cure. Many diseases which take years to develop are never brought to the notice of a doctor until the disease is in an advanced stage. The doctor has then to resort to some violent methods which may only repress the symptoms of the disease and drive it to change its course and develop into something else. People are so accustomed to the prevalent general feeling of ill-health because of their way of living that they may carry quite a serious disease for some time without becoming aware of it.

It will be realised, also, how unfair it is that, although the state does to a certain degree provide free treatment and hospitals for a large number of the people, yet those people are entirely at liberty as to when they choose to use these advantages, and may double the cost and time of cure through ignorant delay.

It will be regarded as wrong that in most cases the life and death of a human being is placed in the hands of one man only—his doctor; and that the doctor's success is jeopardised by the fact that his patient can send for him or not at his own whim. The inadequacy of present arrangements will not be fully perceived until the whole system has been completely revolutionised.

Large institutions will be set up which will take the place of hospitals. They will be built principally for prevention instead of cure. After they have been successfully tried out, such clinics will be erected at set distances apart, to cater for a given number, until every individual of every class has his district institution, or Health-house. Attendance at this Health-house will be strictly compulsory. Once a year or once in six months every person of every age must pass through the building, to be subjected to a complete examination such as is not now known.

He will be examined first in his capacity as an animal, the physical body thoroughly overhauled, and his five senses tested and assessed. He will then be considered in his capacity as a human being, his social success and happiness, his professional work and his family life being given whatever practical psychological aid is indicated. Thirdly, he will be approached in his capacity as an aspiring spiritual individual, and given whatever assistance, comradeship or enlightenment he craves in that way. All these three facets of his make-up will be considered *together,* by experts, in their relationship and reactions to each other. His dossier will be kept, he will be given advice as to diet and any exercises to fit his particular need. It will be compulsory for him to visit the Health-house again at a given date if required to do so.

If this regular supervision is given to a person from babyhood upwards, inhibitions, repressions and bad habits of living and thinking will be largely eliminated as soon as they appear, and a good percentage of diseases will never be able to gain a hold; there will also be a large diminution in the number of crimes. After a few generations of this system so-called 'hereditary' disease will begin to disappear.

The conditions ruling the medical profession itself will also entirely change. The doctor will be a government servant, on a guaranteed salary, and his hours of work will be limited. This will be made possible by a system of group-work for doctors. In each of the Health-houses there will be a group of doctors working as one unit. Each will be medically qualified, but each will specialise to a certain degree. While one, for instance, will concentrate chiefly on the physical body of the patient, a second will centre his attention upon the etheric or radiatory reflexes of the patient, and his glandular reactions to cosmic and local vibrations. A third doctor will consider him from the mental or psychological viewpoint, while a fourth will act more as his spiritual psychologist. Yet another in the group will be available for dietetic knowledge, and the vitally important role of breathing will also receive attention. Each of these doctors will be capable of treating disease as a whole, in the sense that our present general practitioner does, but will have intimate permanent access to the work of his group. The doctors will arrange their work in pairs with shifts, so that regular alternate nights of sleep are assured. The patient will be encouraged to consider his doctor-group as one unit, and to understand how imperative is this all-round treatment.

The Health-house will also be a favourite resort for physical culture of many kinds, with sports and swimming for the athletic-minded, and films, lectures and sermons arranged for the especial needs of patients. Training in cooking and dietetics will be free.

These Health-houses and their organisation will be developed gradually out of experiment, experience and a growing sanity. The enormous accumulation of money, the greater enterprise and mental vitality which will be released, as we have seen, by changing international conditions, will make such innovations possible on a large and thorough scale. Everything will combine to make these changes popular. Improvement and innovation will be, to new and optimistic generations, what pop music and drugs are to be fear-ridden mentalities of today; they will become a national entertainment and necessity.

A citizen of the new era will go into his Health-house with interest, with hope, and with the joy of being thoroughly understood and helped. He will leave it with a new enthusiasm for living, an awakened interest in the gracious art of being at the top of his form, new culinary or gardening tips, and the comfort of knowing the exact state of his own health and the psychological causes of that state.

As generations pass, disease, as we now know it, will rapidly disappear, the professions of surgeon and dentist will no longer be able to exist as single professions, and the ailments of human beings will be practically all psychological. Disease will almost cease to be associated with the Health-houses, which will become pleasure-houses for self-culture and sport and instruction. Finally, they will link up with the colleges and fuse with them into single institutions. This will be because adults, with much time on their hands, will refuse to be debarred from college life and work after they come of age. It will also be considered as extremely wrong to cram young boys and girls with factual knowledge during the years when body and character are being built up, as is done today. From the health point of view education will be changed and modified, and spread out over a much longer period, because it can be continued for as long as required after a profession has been taken up.

In this way youth will cease to be a time of nerve-racking cramming for examinations, occurring mostly during periods of difficult adolescent development which have to be surmounted, not only without adequate spiritual and psychological help, but often when at the mercy of insidious influences. These changes will do much to raise the quality of health and timbre of living far above the level it has reached at this day.

It may seem strange to describe such idyllic conditions of health and living during a time when a large portion of persecuted humanity is forced to roam without education or care of any kind, and when many thousands are enduring an existence similar to that of the pariah dog, right in the midst of so-called civilisation. But here again we must take into account the law of reaction, remembering that the worse any given conditions become, the nearer and more possible is a complete rebound, the swing of the pendulum, and the impulse for reconstruction and regeneration.

The present-day hush-hush policy in relation to illness will soon give way to a more scientific and practical attitude. This will largely be due to a growing public interest in astrology. At present this science is very imperfectly understood, is mostly given out as cheap popular entertainment, and has not yet linked up with medical knowledge. But the study and practice of radiology, the growing knowledge of cosmic and other radiations, and the science of diagnosis and curative treatment through the medium of vibrations are all moving to the point where they will be available for general medical practice. The next step will be to isolate the rays coming from certain planets, determine their chemical influences, and the alterations of these influences according to stellar movements. There, from the medical and orthodox scientific point of view, you will have one aspect of astrology established. Concurrently with this development the public will have passed from its present superficial amusement with newspaper astrology to an independent pursuit of the subject on its own account. As people become more health-conscious so will the health indications of astrology gain their interest, until their findings will coincide with those reached by different methods in medical circles. The hush-hush system will thus naturally be broken down, doctor and patient being able to discuss the condition of the latter on more equal terms, which will make for a more intelligent co-operation.

The progressive heightening of sensitivity among a great many people will bring increasing numbers of cases of 'second sight', principal among these being the power to see the magnetic field set up by an individual, together with the manifold radiations which stream from it, and the various phenomena emanated in the ethers by living beings, often classed under the name of the 'aura'. Auric vision, or etheric vision, will soon be on the increase, and will be accompanied by many ocular afflictions until succeeding generations have become more adjusted to it. Therefore we may look forward to a period which, although it sees the surgeon and the dentist growing rarer, reaps an enormous harvest for the optician, who will have to be extremely highly qualified in the newer vibrationary and radiatory sciences.

Finally, the gross feeding habits of today will soon come to be looked upon with horror. This is already clearly presaged in so many ways. The press is full of salad diets, vitamins and calories. The exemplary diets of those who have had strength to make themselves felt in the world, from dictators to film stars, are becoming such an intrinsic part of their publicity that little imagination is needed to fill in the picture of the future in this respect.

From the present phase of gross, haphazard, ill-chosen and inconsequent feeding the public will, of course, swing in the opposite direction. They will become diet-mad, eating according to astrology, according to vibrations, radiations, the phases of the moon, anything you like! Out of all this experience will come, and people will learn to eat according to the purpose of their lives, and to their especial types. Coming sciences will help them tremendously better to understand this vital subject. The food of the future will be light, delicious, fragrant, largely uncooked and full of sunlight. It will be the fruitarian's dream come true, but with many peculiar additions brought in through radiatory knowledge. The essences of metals will play a considerable part in it. The actual isolation and breathing in of the mineral constituents of the cosmic rays will eventually become one of the higher scientific practices, and this, together with revolutionised astrological knowledge, will open up possibilities to the human being which would only sound like a fairy-tale to poor present-day man.

17

Future Education

As a foil to our vision of coming changes in education we will take a rapid glance at current methods of upbringing.

The object of education up to the present time has been to produce an individual who will be an asset to a sovereign state, or to a country conditioned by a world of sovereign states. He must be reared so that he can be controlled to do the will of his country only, and unquestioningly. It has not been considered safe for him to be acquainted with any point of view outside of and opposed to his own country. Men have, therefore, been brought up in an attitude of bias. Difficult and wearying conditions of living have forced them to accept ready-made ideas. Life, particularly in recent times, has not produced the conditions necessary for individual thinking anywhere. It has been the case of mental survival of only the very fittest! This has meant that at the most one per cent of the public ever achieves an original thought.

People have been brought up with a set of taboos, ideals, and ideas automatically stamped upon them. Almost every individual has been subjected to this same stamping process!

Firstly, he was coloured by the tradition and attitude of his family, possibly by family pride, exclusiveness, greed, possessiveness, ambition, and narrow-mindedness. They made of him a little replica of themselves in as far as they were able. Even the nicest families have their share in the above frailties. On top of these powerful influences the child was hampered not only with inherent health deficiencies, but with those habits of living and feeding which produced them.

Secondly, he was given into the hands of orthodox education. This has been so far completely organised to foster a somewhat blind 'patriotism', in the interests of the state. An extremely biassed history was taught, in which the rest of the world serves only as a foil to the virtue and prowess of his own country. He was imbued with a belief in war, and was trained to consider all people outside his own frontiers as his natural enemies, as 'foreigners', people intrinsically different from himself.

In these ways the attitude of separatism has been built up, and is constantly added to. The individual is asked to subscribe to a hundred 'loyalties'. There is loyalty to his family, to their particular religion and all their fetishes; to his school with its attendant rivalries and separatisms from other schools; to his country as it is represented to him; to the power behind his job, whatever it is; to his club and his social circle; to the exclusiveness found even in the realm of his hobby or sport; and to the political party with which he takes sides. So, loyalty within loyalty crowds his life, until his every thought and instinct is bound and defined ready-made by one of them.

What actually are all these loyalties? They are grooves of thought planned and built up, even if unconsciously, by those people who wish to gain and keep a hold upon the individual, either for his vote, his labour, his money, his influence, or his support. Some of them may be right and worthy, some of them not so, but the fact of their purpose and effect remains.

So, firstly through family influence, and secondly through educational and propagandist influences, his attitude of separatism is strongly built up.

The third influence is that of economic necessity.

The individual of today is brought up in an atmosphere of fear and apprehension. He is faced with the prospect of 'earning his own living' in a world which, although it claims his every loyalty, may nevertheless have no use for him. If he belongs to the few who are born with good incomes, then he still may be in perpetual apprehension as to his ability to keep it, his fear of making false moves, or of managing his family life unwisely, or of parting with too much of it to the myriad demands made upon him by those anxious to get it away from him for good reasons or bad. Added to this, the affairs of the world are now in such a chaotic state that no one can be sure of his financial future any longer.

Therefore, from the highest to the lowest, the life of the individual is influenced by fear or dread, which naturally inhibits him in all phases of his outlook. This fear usually persists throughout life, because in any case it becomes part of the fabric of his character. This terrible heritage of fear is due also to the crime of separatism, and the fact that life between nation, between class and company, is competitive and rivalrous, producing an uneven sharing out of land and of material and of opportunity in a world of plenty.

The individual is, therefore, brought up at present in the thrall of a vicious circle. His upbringing prevents him from being capable of constructive clear thinking, and his world is in a mess because of the need of such thinking. He has been firstly educated to regard himself as a member and a perquisite of his family, then as a member and a perquisite of his country. He is never represented to himself as a member of world humanity, with the freedom of the world as his heritage.

Patriotism has proved to be a wonderful inspiration throughout history, ennobling life and urging men to progress and fulfilment. But, after all, patriotism is actually devotion to an ideal. Whether the devotion is to one's country or to one's continent, or to all one's fellow men does not make such a difference as we at first sight might suppose. The difference is that the scope is larger, the vision greater, and the possible results relatively grander. The fact that the taint of possessiveness which marks national patriotism would be missing in world patriotism, as would also be the vice of separatism, puts world patriotism nearer to true Christianity than the lesser attribute which has served us until now.

The development of education will move forward under the

same influences which bring such radical changes in other walks of life. Men's interests will be focused upon World Unity, synthesised economics, international fusions and amalgamations of a hundred kinds. In measure as it becomes demonstrated how much social conditions are going to benefit from the new enterprises of breaking down international barriers of all sorts it will become necessary to educate people to support these activities. World history, world economics, and international relationships of every kind will be studied. The mark of a good education will be to show the capacity for liking, understanding and valuing any and every nation. The future type of patriot will desire his country to play an exemplary part in international living. His personal ambition will be worthily to fill the role of world citizen.

An international language, to be learnt as a child, as well as one's native tongue, will, of course, become the obvious necessity, and will almost certainly be the English language.

Probably the most popular study in colleges will be that of international economics. This will include the many problems engaging the minds of branches of the international governing bodies, such as that of the control of food supplies, now freed from any tariffs or customs, their growth and distribution, so that everyone obtains fair treatment, and all that is required. To this end the study of solar, lunar and planetary influences, and of recurring cycles in regard to crops will play a big part.

Another popular study will centre round money and currencies, which will be subjected to many drastic experiments, the final aim being to substitute barter or exchange of goods in as many instances as possible. Profit and interest on money transactions will become unpopular, and a new system of commerce quite different to anything before tried will come into use. This will necessitate the study of a new arithmetic, based not on addition and subtraction, but upon horizontal distribution.

The study of metaphysics will become obligatory and will embrace the scientific aspects of the whole trend of evolution. An intense and ardent study of the mind will absorb many students. The actual development of mind-power as a force able to control physical matter will come into the school curriculum. The vast subject of vibrationary and radiatory life, and of electrical and magnetic phenomena will produce many branches of learning. People will become fully aware of the law of similarity of vibration, the law of which we spoke in connection with Meditation and which maintains that a given thought, held with sufficient power, creates a form in the ether which acts as a receiving station to similar vibrations. Thus by holding such a thought steadily information regarding its subject flows continuously into the mind.

This will constitute one of the fundamental changes in education. Instead of cramming the pupil with facts, he will be asked to give information himself about a quite unfamiliar subject. He will have to exercise his mind in the way described, and write down all that comes to him. This will be the elementary stage of mental training. The more advanced stage will demand that the pupil practises reasoning, deduction and analogy around a given subject until he produces an original idea or a creative suggestion with regard to it. Creative thought will take the place of memory by degrees, until mental capabilities develop to results which we of the present day could hardly understand.

There are many experiments moving in these directions already extant, such as Pelmanism and some of the newer forms of education. Actually it will mean that the mind will be brought into use, instead of the brain, as it is today. In time general creative thinking will be achieved, so that every individual can play his part in world affairs.

Some of the mental exercises will be fraught with danger, as for instance that of 'keeping an open mind'. An open mind can not only receive anything, it can also lose everything. The old danger of the separatist's closed mind will give place to a condition which may be carried to excess with equally stupefying results. The growing interest in second sight, or the capacity to see the activities of the higher dimensional worlds, will reach such proportions that it will acquire the nature of a craze, an obsession, or a vice, playing somewhat the part that alcoholism now does. Educational authorities will have to tackle this matter very seriously, training the young to get their values right and to have a legitimate scientific interest equally in all the spheres open to their senses. It is indeed difficult to talk of many of men's future interests, as they are hardly imaginable to us today, involving, as they will, the development of responses to stimuli so delicate, and colours so translucent, and vibrations so subtle that scientific instruments are not now able to detect them.

Telepathy and thought-reading will be studied as a matter of course. Children will at an early age be able to send and receive telepathic messages. There will come a time when men's thoughts may with difficulty be hidden from their companions, but at that far-distant age morality will so have progressed that dissimulation would have little purpose.

Men will become so absorbed by the growing comprehension of the potentialities of their own minds that outer forms of entertainment such as we now enjoy will largely lose their appeal. The all-absorbing occupation will be 'What can I do with my mind? Can I revive dying creatures with its radiations, or make my flowers and plants to prosper, or to take on new colours? Can I link with any of the hidden mentalities who are busy with the Creator's work and plans? Can I stimulate the mind of my dear neighbour which is not as strong as my own? Can I direct love to a tribe still left in a distant part of the world who are less advanced than ourselves?'

Future education will include a considerable array of knowledge which would be new to us today. The psychological influence of colours will be deeply studied, and their scientific use in art, in decoration, and in healing will be seriously developed. The art of the future will be created by mental sensitivity to effect mental response, instead of, as hitherto, being created by emotional feeling to create emotional reaction. The difference here may not at first be apparent. Emotions react to the third-dimensional life, that of body and brain, and to outward beauty, to love, to suffering, to bravery and all the other 'animal' attributes. The mind, on the contrary, responds to fourth-dimensional and even fifth-dimensional life, to the causes instead of the effects, to the underlying forces at work, to the problems, wonders, patterns, ideals, plans and organisations which build up the universe. The mind appreciates colour, not sensuously, but as a certain force or quality possessing many attributes, and giving the key and the clue to the purpose of various manifestations.[1]

The same developments will take place in the realm of music. The new music will appeal to the mind instead of to the emotions, and will portray the life which underlies physical form, and the entities and forces which are at work and at play in fourth-dimensional radiatory matter. A foretaste of this music has already been given to us by several composers such as Ravel. The very obvious musical forms (distinct motifs in separative compartments) which have described third-dimensional life up till now have clearly given way to a fusing, blending, accidental type of musical form which describes the radiatory world, the elements, the elemental creatures of nature, and the intersecting of many rays, cosmic, macrocosmic and microcosmic, from the thought of a God to the passions of forest creatures, from the beams of a planet to the radiations from a mortal being. The music of Wagner will live longer than most other music of the third-dimensional age, for the reason that he did try to depict cosmic happenings, and to bring a conception of the vastness of the universe and the panorama of evolution on to his musical canvas.

Most astonishing of all, perhaps, will be the developments with regard to perfume. Some remarkable discoveries will be made in relation to this phenomenon which will be enhanced by men's growing sensitivity to it, and the strong reactions which it will evoke. The science of perfumes will become a profound and a popular one. The fact, already known, that a certain note of music has a close relationship to a certain colour and perfume will be the foundation for the future

[1] See *The Finding of the Third Eye.*

science of the senses. In time, music will be performed in company with its colour and perfume complements. The practice of listening to music in a blaring, crude-coloured, brightly lit concert hall as we do today would be dismissed as a barbaric impossibility.

The blending of certain perfumes, colours and musical tones will be used therapeutically, as anaesthetics, for healing, for muscular development, for the expansion of the mind-cells, and for many other purposes. Already today kindred methods are being successfully tried out. Future education, largely concerned with such delicate and delightful studies and experiments, will have much of beauty and of joy in it.

The study of rays, of their interaction, of crystal and other pattern formations brought about in the ethers, and of their respective planetary influences, will be a favourite one. Added to this will be the study of the rays sent out by the mind, of their intersecting with emotional rays to form crystal patterns in the body, and of the way in which destructive separative thinking can thus cause a disease. It will become possible to film the reactions of dislike and fear upon the body cells. The regular showing of such films will provide an object lesson well calculated to foster an excellent control of the mind, and of evil habits.

It may be thought that this picture of future education represents an enormous amount of complicated study to be encompassed. A few generations hence, because of the changing conditions we have foretold, the human mind will be a reservoir of so much energy, and of such rapidly working powers, that present-day education would suffice only for a future kindergarten stage. Besides which, the whole methods of teaching and assimilation will be entirely different. The child will be told what there is to learn, and the reasons for learning it, and, once imbued with an eager ambition, the teaching process will consist mostly of actual mind-training, of a kind we do not now know. The rest will be left to the child itself. Certain questions will be put to the child, who will proceed to instruct the teacher upon them! And the teacher will actually give profound attention, in the hope of gaining new information, should the child's capacity for mental tuning-in prove to be stronger than his own. 'And a little child shall lead them . . .' 'Until ye become as little children . . .' will later be understood as true scientific prophecy.

We have now touched upon many of the changes which the process known as education will undergo. A few of them will have their inception well before the end of this century.

Of these changes the most fundamental will be in the attitude towards education itself. The latter process has hitherto been applied largely as a method whereby facts are reiterated by the older generation to the younger, until some of them have made a fairly lasting impression upon the phenomenon known as memory. Adult people teach and train children and teach and train animals in the hope of bringing them up to be good and useful members of the community. The idea that the teacher could learn anything from his pupils, whether human or animal, has never entered into the scheme of things at all. This has been due to the reign of separatism and the cultivation of the autocratic sentiment reflected from the sovereign government right down into the humblest teacher's mind; it has been due to the lack of that spirit of fusion and unity with all things, which, as the fourth dimension ripens, will radically change the human approach to 'education'.

It will begin to be recognised that although the body and brain of a child is new and young, its subconscious, its sensitivities, its etheric and mental apparatus may be quite adult; and its soul, or superconscious, even more so. It will be appreciated that the upbringing of a child consists in helping an entity, who may be of any age or quality, to learn to use a new and growing physical apparatus, and to condition itself to environments with which it may or may not be familiar. The parent or teacher will come to realise that in measure as the body is new and ignorant, so may there be qualities of vision, of memory and of deduction from which much could be learnt by the more crystallised adult. The child will be treated not only as an equal, but as a mysterious source of knowledge, possibly superior to that of his elder, who may have lost his facility for 'tuning-in'. In this way a new, intimate and absorbing relationship will spring up between the child and the adult which will effect a mutual stimulation and banish the prevailing attitude of impatient autocracy for ever.

It will be borne in mind that any child may, fifty years later, have become a genius, a leader of men; that the potentialities of that character, its knowledge and its power, are already there, linked to it as a part of itself, lying beneath the third-dimensional threshold, and able to be reached by certain means. The impersonal love which brings radiation and understanding will give the clue to these means, which are impossible of attainment today because of the non-existence to any degree of the capacity for that impersonal love!

Take the case of animals also. People, through the latter quality, will appreciate the fact that an animal's lack of ability to speak the human tongue reduces nothing of its other powers; of the world of knowledge in which it lives, hidden from us, and of the many things it sees, senses and knows, to which we are blind and insensitive. Earnestly as future man will seek to learn from the child, he will strive even more ardently to learn from the animal, the bird and the insect, and to penetrate the life and knowledge enjoyed by kingdoms other than his own.

Thus, in future days, it will be the adult who will be learning all his life, childhood and adolescence being reserved mostly for training and growing the physical, moral and mental apparatus. Instead of implying, as now, to the child: 'You will have to work hard, learn a lot, go to school, and then afterwards you will be grown-up and free of all that drudgery', the prospect held up to the future child will be: 'You must first acquire perfection, health and discipline of the body, the emotions and the brain, so that when the growing process is completed you will be able to enjoy the thrill of acquiring knowledge to your heart's content.'

There will be so much more time for it all than there now is. Science will have halved the needed hours of human labour, so that the use of the leisure of adult beings will be a bigger problem by far than that of the child. People will not grow old in the way that they now do. They will come to believe that the course of 'education' and development will be unbroken by physical death. So the incentive and capacity for study and creative work will remain undimmed throughout life, and there will always be enough time for both study and professional work to run concurrently.

It can thus be seen that in the future the influence of radiation and synthesis will affect education so that it ceases to be a separative section of adolescent life, but merges with the entire existence of the adult; finally blending, as we have seen, in our consideration of the 'Health-house' system, with his health-culture, and with what remains of hospital and medical treatment.

We must remember, also, that the aspect of living which we now know under the separative title of 'religion' will become the worship of the Creator and His Mind as It plays through all aspects of life and of knowledge, from its stance as the head and fountain of all education. For of course the new education will finally be able to come completely into line with the emerging true Christianity. It will at last be sought fully to obey, not only the Ten Commandments, but their amplification through the injunctions of Christ Himself. Thus the churches and the educational institutions will be drawn into ever closer co-operation, the findings of scientists and intellectuals being brought as thank-offering to the church and interpreted from the pulpit.

If we are able to vision church and college working together in this way, teaching a mode of life from which dogma, bigotry, nationalism, class-consciousness and all separativeness is banished, and the new genius of group-work has entered in, we shall appreciate the amazingly different conditions upon which future generations will be able to build their lives.

18

The Pre-Golden Age

We cannot be definite about the time it will take for the Golden Age, the flower of the new civilisation, to mature. Much history, on a small scale such as that of the last thousand years, will continue to be made, so that the broader changes taking place will be veiled by smaller detail. Perhaps if we were to look clearly ahead into the Golden Age itself most of what we saw would appear incomprehensible to us, because of our ignorance of the developments which led up to it. Let us therefore attempt to vision a period midway between the present day and the full flowering of the future civilisation, and obtain an idea of the development of average living conditions.

The impulses of men all this while will have been moving towards the coherent fusion of all aspects of life, the elimination of all unnecessary details and activities, the simplifying and beautifying of all necessities. We have already seen the anticipation of this in modern building, lighting and decoration. All the fussy detail, dark heavy colouring and infinite complications to be found in the homes of the passing age have made way for a new spirit which craves bare plain surfaces, delicate luminous colours, simple labour-saving arrangements, scarcity of ornaments and mystery and discretion in lighting. This new spirit banishes sentimentality but not sentiment. To the emotional it appears hard because it throws the cold light of reason on inherited inhibitions and habits and says '*Why* must we have this and that?' It is the first sign of the genius of individual mental activity coming into being, the genius of the instinct to expand, to broaden the capacity for vision and knowledge. The passing age was not ready to take in broader vision, so it restricted its focus by hemming itself in with myriads of little details and possessions. Humanity was still a child, afraid of growing up.

But the coming of humanity's adulthood is upon us. It will bring a complete *volte-face*. 'Clear the way! We are taking on responsibility now! We want to see exactly where we are going!' And so away will go all the old ruts, habits, separatisms, possessivenesses in all aspects of men's lives, the change showing most clearly in his conception of house and home.

The house has already largely given way to the flat-building. People have been unbelievably ready to give up the sovereignty of the detached house and join in a life which is becoming ever more communal. They share heating, water, service, gardens and other amenities between quite a colony of families in the large apartment buildings. This is only the prelude to what is coming.

Housing conditions will change more and more, both under the influence of the new dispensation and of the new inventions. Heating and lighting facilities will be utterly different as soon as the new electricity is under control. Entire streets or great blocks will be built as one unit, heated and lit from one source. Refuse, laundry, milk and other of the common services will be run pneumatically through passages in the walls. Much traffic will pass deep underground. Roof space will be flat, and comprise the whole top surface of the block. This will all be utilised as children's playgrounds, sports-grounds, pleasure grounds and salad gardens. Bridges will communicate from roof to roof, so that the acreage of the town will be duplicated. A group of these blocks will house a community as nearly self-supporting as possible, and be surrounded by a considerable portion of cultivated ground. Big cities will be converted into linked garden towns, each supplying sufficient work for its inhabitants. People will be encouraged to live within walking distance of their work. The present-day unhealthy habit of rushing through miles of tube railway or congested streets to one's daily work will be entirely abolished.

Coal and other forms of smoke-producing fuel will no longer be allowed. The atmosphere in towns will be clean and pure, so that intensive vegetable and salad cultivation will be possible on a large portion of the town roof surface.

Sunlight will no longer be kept out by tall buildings. They will be manufactured out of a material like glass, allowing the passage of the healthy sunlight rays, yet being opaque to the vision. Into this building material a newly invented substance will be introduced which absorbs sunlight by day and radiates it back softly after dark, thus ensuring a minimum light and warmth during the twenty-four hours. There will be no such thing as a dark sombre room either by day or night. Houses will glow like the inside of a flower, or a sea-shell, in the sun. This effect will be so beautiful and so stimulating that little in the way of furniture or ornamentation will be needed. The mode of having dozens of upright chairs and tables in a room will pass away. The tables and seating accommodation will be part of the room itself, supplemented by hassock cushions upon the floor. There will be no need to 'move the chair near to the fire or window' as light and warmth will be all-pervading.

Habits of hygiene will improve in measure with other things. It will not be allowed to step from outdoors into a house without changing the shoes. Usually a very light sandal will be worn, and this will be exchanged for a house-sandal on entering the home. These sandals will be constructed of synthetic material, and will be beautifully made and decorated by a member of the household. The craving for articles of quality and workmanship will grow ever more imperative. Creative handicraft will come right to the foreground of domestic life, to the benefit and joy of everyone concerned. People will take pride in making beautiful things of everyday use and in exchanging them for the work of their friends. For a variety of reasons furs will lose their popularity. The thick fur coat will appear too clumsy to the future lovers of form and colour, and too heavy for their more highly toned bodies. There will be other and more subtle reasons also, having to do with future relationships with animals and sensitivity to certain vibrations.

People's sense of values will change very decidedly. They will care for what they can express with their person or talents more than for outward show of opulence. Their pride will not be in possessing a Rolls-Royce or the entrance to a snobbish club, but in expressing original and perfect taste and sense of beauty in every single article of apparel or of use with which they are equipped. This will be the natural result of un-harassed leisure and warm vitality. Such things as cheap wholesale manufactured goods would be abhorred. There will be an intelligent and practical preference for a single fine hand-made long-wearing article instead of for one of inferior cheap quality which has to be replaced a dozen times. Garments will have an astrological basis for their colour and design and express the intrinsic character of their wearer. The soothing influence of handicraft will allay the unappeased feverish restlessness which lack of creative work entails in all people. The love of speed and noise will thus die a natural death, and everyone will begin to savour the delights which lurk in all the little 'humdrum' duties of daily life. Much less food will be eaten, but its understanding and preparation will become a fascinating art. People will want to participate in the growing of the things they eat. This will become a psychic necessity to them.

In these ways town and country will draw ever closer together, the towns becoming 'countrified', and the country absorbing more and more of town amenities and culture. Travelling facilities will of course increase with future inventions, distances being successively annihilated by various means.

One of the later discoveries will make it possible for a person to fly without an aeroplane or any visible or cumbersome contraption. The bombardments of radium and the disruption of the atom will have something to do with this invention. A man will have a small container attached to him, which includes a mechanism by whose means he can set a chemical action in process which will release electrons from disintegrating atoms at such a speed that the power set free will be sufficient to propel him through the air. But it would be a matter of a hair's-breadth for the energy released to blow him into a thousand pieces instead! So terrible dangers will have to be lived through before this invention is well under control.

Men will learn a vast amount more about the cosmic rays. Their growing powers of communication with animal life, which will of course be within the realm of vibrations, something resembling semaphore, helped by telepathy, will give them a clue to possible means of communicating with beings of whose existence upon or within some of the planets they feel convinced. The hope of setting up communications with life outside the earth's radius will become an evergrowing desire. Many experiments will be made, many false hopes raised, much exploitation will prosper, before men's understanding will reach a point where they will be better able to encompass this desire. No instruments or machines will avail them. They will finally realise, after many generations have been practising various forms of mind-control, that if a group of people could project their minds *together* as one mind to the particular planet they wish to contact, the channel formed would be strong enough to act as a 'television', allowing them to gain admittance by mental wireless, as it were, to the planet, and impress their own visit upon the life there as well. This 'magic' of the future will become so absorbing and dangerous a game that many will unfortunately lose their minds over it, thus adding to the subtle mental diseases of the day. Like spiritualism, this practice will be bitterly accused because the wrong people are able to take part in it.

As the wonders of life open up before men the possibilities brought to light will somewhat overbalance many of them. Instead of today's appalling death-rate from such monstrosities as cancer, strange new nervous diseases will make their appearance due to people's inability to adjust themselves to the higher tempos of life and to the changes taking place within themselves. Most of the mental diseases and nervous disorders of today are due to fear, restriction, disappointment and boredom. Those of the future period at which we are now looking will be due to exactly opposite causes. The lack of fear and restriction will sometimes bring on a type of nervous abandon unknown to us today. The glorious spiritual vision and certainty which will open out before men will often be too much for the physical brain to stand, while the tremendous mental stimulation under which they will exist will frequently make a too intensive demand upon the channels of nerve force. The endocrine glands will be intensely affected as they respond more and more to the subtler vibrations. All of them will undergo new interactions and readjustments and developments.

The adrenals will have to cope with a tremendous acceleration of 'energy traffic'. They will have to develop a much more intensive interaction with the thyroid and particularly the para-thyroid glands.

The solar plexus responses and reflexes will take place consciously instead of unconsciously, that area becoming like a telephone exchange to all the cosmic vibrations to which man will become individually sensitive. The solar plexus will come into much closer co-operation with the pituitary gland. This latter will produce increasingly conscious reactions to certain sections of the ether to which we have already referred, those strata which reflect images from many sources. Today some of these reactions go under the name of psychometry and clairvoyance, but they are the exception and not the rule.

Men will become alive to the fact that the heart has very important functions other than that of beating. The heart's action will cease to be an involuntary one and come under the conscious control of the will. The close connection between breathing and thinking, as well as the great variety of chemical reactions produced by different types of breathing, together with the all-important channel of thought which resides in the heart, will become part of man's conscious equipment. An intensive interaction between the heart and the Pineal gland will be developed, leading to spiritual vision, knowledge and first-hand experience of the hidden worlds, which will utterly change the focus of men's consciousness and of their life-motive.

All these potent and startling developments will produce a temporary strain upon humanity which will be a heavy one to bear, bringing about many peculiar aberrations. Extreme exhaustion and over-stimulation will result in states of coma, complete immobility, trances, split personalities, various severe eye troubles, and finally a curious disease in which the patient is continually confused between two worlds, that of waking and that of sleeping.

None of these afflictions will be considered, as they would be today, to be symptoms of insanity or mental inefficiency. They will be understood for what they are. They will be intelligently cured by a system of 'mental massage and gymnastics' designed to soothe and to strengthen those particular organs of perception which are over-strained. Finally a law will be passed enforcing a period of isolated rest and seclusion for every individual once a year. This will be taken in specially constructed rest-homes upon islands reserved for this purpose. Before long the responses to this treatment will be so remarkable and so inspiring that many people will look upon it as the great treat and opportunity of the year.

The heightened sensitivities of the masses will cause them to feel completely stifled if herded in large crowds as they are today. Instead of feeling that a great concourse is an ingredient of festivity, they will discover that only in small gatherings can they sense and enjoy their own reactions. They will not care to be lost in mass hypnotism and reaction, preferring to respond on their individual initiative. The mass response will gradually become mental instead of emotional.

This will result in a gradual dying-out of partisanship, of prejudice and of fanaticism. The general attitude to the matter in hand will be that which is only attempted at the present day by the magistrate and the judge. People will feel convicted of mental inferiority if they cannot completely identify themselves with the point of view of each opposing faction. It will no longer be considered the thing to 'have an opinion'. A dislike, or a definite opinion, will be regarded as a restriction and a limitation, because people will come to realise that their real aim is to know truth, and that the truth about anything or anyone is a fluid quality. It differs according to the angle of viewpoint, according to person and circumstance. It changes continuously and for everyone. Therefore to have an opinion (in the sense in which that is done today) will be considered static, stagnant, mentally unclean, and unimportant. To have knowledge, on the other hand, to respond to truth, and to hope to acquire wisdom and identification with reality, will be the earnest ambition of the average man.

The conditions of living in a world which is no longer possessive or opinionated, and in which class and age set up no barriers, are hard to picture. We may say: 'Oh, this savours of socialism, equality for all, which can never succeed because there must always be the intellectual and the labouring types, the leaders and the followers.' Indeed, this will continue to be so, and each man will be given work suited to his type. But no one will be *only* an intellectual, or only a labourer, or only a leader or a follower. The intellectual will have a part of his time spent on manual outdoor work, the secondary work of the labourer will be concerned with art or literature. The leader of men will always procure for a hobby something for which he has little aptitude and where he is under another's command. The lowliest labourer will be encouraged to excel in some little hobby, and, through it, teach or lead others.

In these ways wise authority will provide against any member of the community leading unfulfilled, unbalanced or cramped lives. The labourer will never be discontented or stupefied, the leader will not grow autocratic. The niche which each one fills will have its charm and its importance.

As we earlier saw, this principle will also be applied to nations who, although federated together in a unified life, will have each their special qualities and capacities brought out to the utmost. Rivalry will not exist, nor competition, because the contribution of each nation will be found to be intrinsically different, and essential to the whole.

A citizen of the future will not vaguely feel, as would his counterpart today, that a person of another nationality is a 'foreigner', a chap who is 'somehow' different or 'somehow' rather the same as himself! He will seek with understanding to enjoy those particular racial gifts which are different to his own, realising that he depends upon them to fill certain gaps in his own life, and that the intimate exchange of friendship between nationals of different countries actually provides a subtle kind of nourishment unobtainable in any other way.

Men will learn to appraise each other and work together from the standpoint of their astrological or vibrationary make-up. In the same way the stellar rulership of nations will begin to be understood, and their individual genius and destiny thus revealed. It will then be no more possible to think of crushing out, incapacitating or suppressing a nation than it would be to think of deliberately cutting off, crippling or tying up one of one's own limbs; it will appear just as foolish.

Thus the laws of fusion and unity will gradually filter into men's consciousness, and into their outward living, bringing not the bugbear which we now fear—loss of individuality and initiative—but a freer and a heightened individuality, unwarped by our famous inferiority complex, dignified and natural in the expression of its own acknowledged genius and essentiality.

So far we have visioned a future expressing changes which are hard for us at this day to picture or to savour. A world from which fear, want, physical disease, partisanship and enmity have largely disappeared is difficult to imagine. A way of life in which love plays the chief part and governs the world opens up before us. But it is to be an unemotional, impartial, impersonal, all-embracing love, of a kind which we do not know and could hardly understand today, the real Christ-love of identification with all of life.

We have glimpsed far ahead of us a physical life which is

luminous, leisured and quiet compared in many respects with our own. Our present 'commodities', such as coal, gas, steam and oil, together with all the unpleasant labour, dirt, noise and smell which they entail, are destined to become completely obsolete and forgotten. The present crush and rush and roar of traffic will come to be a horror of the past. Goods will be blown along in pneumatic passages underground! Passengers will be very few in number, as walking will be preferred, or else riding upon something which will resemble a very light electric scooter, and which can be folded and carried upon the arm like an umbrella. As for umbrellas, they will have gone out of fashion. All clothes will be weatherproofed by a new process, and people will have learnt to value the beautifying and tonic properties of rain.

While the art of physical life will lie in simplifying every need, the opposite will apply to mental needs, as they become ever more vital, intense and searching. The era of so-called magic will dawn, when the true powers of the mind come to be understood and demonstrated; a strange world in which the inventions of science are continually being ousted by men's own growing personal powers. For instance, the triumph of scientists when they finally teach men how to fly individually and without wings will be short-lived. People will suddenly discover that it is not so necessary to take their bodies everywhere with them, and that they can accomplish some errands through a process of personal mind-projection or human television.

Experiments in this latter practice will bring to light curious phenomena regarding its effect when carried out in groups. A wonderful secret concerning the human alchemy of scientifically arranged group-work will come to light. After this, things will be possible of accomplishment which will even astonish our 'magic-minded' descendants!

Let us next contemplate, if we can, the working of the mind of such a descendant, a man living a hundred years hence, secure in the fullness of the new civilisation, and standing upon the threshold of the Golden Age.

19

Men's Minds in A.D. 2070

The future of men's minds is known to their superconscious, and reflected from it into their subconscious, usually without making any impression upon the brain at all. In the same way the memory of the past development of the human mind is stored within the subconscious. The psycho-analyst has demonstrated how much lies buried beneath the threshold of everyday consciousness. This treasure-store consists very largely of knowledge concealed in symbols, numbers, signs and patterns, in conjunction with which colour often plays an important part. Much of this stored material is atavistic, or has to do with the past, but often clear cases of prevision have been uncovered and substantiated. Therefore we know that the human ego is linked with both past and future along channels which need not necessarily impinge upon the brain at all.

What do we exactly mean when we speak of the super-conscious and of the subconscious? The opinions of average experimentalists in these regions always seem a little vague. So we must be sure of arriving at a clear definition. We recently described man as a threefold being, comprising 'animal man', 'human man', and 'spiritual man'. I should say that the so-called subconscious comprises the knowledge and memory of all that appertains to animal man; that the average brain-consciousness embraces all that concerns the life of the human man; and that the superconscious is man's channel or link with the spiritual realm, or world of causes, wherein is pictured the plan and purpose of world history from the beginning to the end. We can understand in this way how, through his human side, man is in interaction with the physical world of the lower three dimensions; how, through his animal nature, when properly developed, he is in interaction with the fourth-dimensional world of vibrations and radiations, which play through the ethers—just as animals are— and gains in the same way his guiding 'instincts', which are responses to natural laws; and how, through his spiritual nature, as soon as he can tune up to it, he is in interaction with the fifth-dimensional world of plan, of cause, and of pattern, wherein is shown life as a whole, past, present and future, and time no longer exists in its lower-dimensional sense. In this realm, time, instead of spreading out through space, is converging into the great withinness of which we spoke, and thus past, present and future have come together, presenting one completed picture. When man can link successfully with his superconscious he obtains infinitesimal flashes of this completed picture of truth, which result in what we call intuition.

We now come to an interesting point. So long as man remains pre-eminently *human man* he has to rely for his knowledge upon *memory,* that is to say upon those facts which have been imprinted upon his physical brain since birth. His knowledge, therefore, consists of a mass of facts, statements and ideas communicated to him through other human beings. As soon as he is able to contact for himself, through concentration, meditation or contemplation, either deliberate or involuntary, dimensions higher than the physical he begins to obtain first-hand information. He obtains this information in a realm not constricted to words, nor conditioned by time. This means that he can learn to obtain information *instantaneously,* and eventually upon any subject. This means that *memory,* as we know it, is no longer so necessary! Men will come to realise that instead of having their brains packed with an assortment of facts which they may or may not need, it is better to train the powers of the mind, to develop concentration and one-pointedness (or the power of tuning up to a certain vibration and sounding it forth steadily for as long as desired, thus contacting everything of affinity with it) so that they can at any time contact instantaneously any knowledge which they definitely require.

This may sound a fantastic accomplishment. But man does it at the present time. *Only,* so far he can tune in merely to those vibrations which have already been imprinted upon his brain. Someone says: '—cornfield—', for instance. The word sounds its vibration, or number, and the tuning-fork in his brain responds by pouring forth in a flood of 'memory' all which was impressed upon it under that particular vibration. Enough to fill a book may be rapidly called forth. Where does it all come from?

However, in this case man will learn nothing new about 'cornfield'—he will only mentally reiterate facts that have been stored. Whereas if, instead of using the receptive attitude, he learns deliberately to set up a certain vibration and hold it poised long enough, he will be able to *draw* to him (which is a positive and not a receptive action) much knowledge which is new to him.

This practice will constitute a large part of men's future mental training, and will take the place of memory. This is one of the fundamental differences between the mind of the future and that of today. Memory will gradually come to be considered as a primitive attribute used by the masses, while the intelligentsia employ a less cumbersome road to knowledge.

Eventually, of course, knowledge through meditation will come to be the universal method.

In measure as men develop their powers of meditation or mind-control much astonishing information will be available to them. The power to contact the past will be used by advanced men, in the fifth dimension, where the actual plan and pattern of evolution is held poised. Men of lesser calibre will tune in to the 'cinematograph' of events past and present which is held by the reflective quality of a stratum of the ether. The fact that a vast majority of people in history have believed in rebirth or reincarnation will come to be explained. Men, visioning many scenes in the past, will begin to gain a much broader view upon the whole subject. They will see life as continuous evolution, in which the one quality most clearly progressing is individuality. They will learn that individuality is only built up through long aeons of experience and evolution, and that therefore an outstanding example of individuality (whether of human character, or any other expression of life) is an example of great age. They will thus learn that a certain part of themselves must be of very ancient origin, and that their *individual* reactions to various aspects of life *must* have been built up in similar circumstances throughout very long periods of time. In many ways they will come to learn the true situation as applied to the question of reincarnation. Their whole view upon this subject will broaden enormously, becoming a thing of experience and not of surmise.

Through their growing intimacy with animal life men will learn much about planetary and cosmic rays and radiations. They will discover how all things come under the radiatory rulership of various of these rays, to the degree that they may be said to be expressions of them in physical matter. Their growing sensitivities will enable them to associate themselves with their own ruling rays and thus to set up a conscious link with the forces at work within their own lives. They will come to realise that the *individuality* or innateness of aspects of their 'spiritual' knowledge and of their soul-character has been built up through aeons of experience upon or within other spheres than that of the earth, either of one of the known planets, or of globes unknown perhaps even to average astrologists. They will learn that 'reincarnation' does not only constitute cyclic reappearance upon this earth, but upon other globes or spheres of life as well. Like an insect emerging from a cocoon their minds will come out of a tiny prison of darkness into a world of illumination and of possibilities of endless horizon. Consciousness will be released from its focus in the flesh, and will find itself free in the fifth dimension, the Kingdom of Heaven, borne thereto in the arms of Love, the radiations of the fourth dimension, veiling the Heart of Christ.

Men will not be content with intimacy with animal life only. The mineral and the vegetable kingdoms will claim their earnest courtship as well. Even at the present day scientists are becoming dimly aware of the sensitive individuality which informs an atom, a cell, a piece of metal or a plant. All of these are now known to breathe, to discriminate, to suffer pain and pleasure, fatigue and stimulation. Their intensive reactions to a vast number of radiations are even now suspected. The supposition that the amazing 'instincts' which guide beast, bird and insect may in reality be conscious intelligent responses to information conveyed by radiations, sometimes over immense distances, has already been put forward. It has been suspected that living 'wireless receivers' to these radiations are carried by all creatures in the form of hair, feather and antenna. The next step will be a strong realisation of the creative, intelligent living consciousnesses which move, thinly veiled, beneath the physical forms of animal, vegetable and mineral life. As soon as the existence of these brilliant intelligences becomes established in the consciousness of men they will never rest until they have set up some communication with them. This they will succeed in doing through the medium of radiations. They will discover and locate certain of the radiations which creatures in the 'lower' kingdoms use for intercommunication. They will endeavour to send messages to them, and to receive some of their own communications. These will at first be picked up on fine instruments, which will later be dispensed with as man himself grows more radiatorily sensitive.

From sources such as these men will learn a tremendous number of illuminating facts about the varying contents of the atmosphere around them, and the possibility of drawing certain types of nourishment from it by employing various rhythms in breathing, and in posture. They will learn why a snake coils, why a bird sings and why he stands on one leg to sleep, why a flower wears a certain colour, and what are the rays which inform a diamond. They will learn that each of these mysteries bears an application to themselves which can enhance their own powers of living. They will come to believe, also, in the vital and honourable part which mankind is called upon to play in regard to the lower kingdoms. Men will begin to regard themselves as occupying a peculiarly responsible position in the make-up of the universe. They will consider themselves as the great link between divine and material manifestation, the interpreter and mediator between one kingdom and another; standing as pupils and aspirants to divinity, and as teachers and deities to the lower kingdoms. The complete interdependence of this design and plan will become apparent to them. Henceforth a thinking man will hold himself with the same dignity, care and responsibility as a king or president must do *vis-à-vis* his dependent subjects today. He will come to consider himself as an infinitesimal creature bearing yet the germ of a growing God within his breast, Who must one day rule a planet or direct a constellation. In this conception man's courage must equal his humility. When men reach the stage of having their great destiny thus revealed to them it will be because humanity has at last left its adolescence and has passed into adulthood. At that stage they will discover for themselves the existence of a vast community of beings sharing with them the building and development of evolution on this planet. These beings, great and small, belong to what is known as the Deva Kingdom. Their existence and their work is complementary to mankind's, and co-operation with them brings great bliss.

How different will the mind of future man be to our own, when it is reared in such lofty conceptions! How fascinating will his interests be, and how little will petty personalities and importances have power to move him. Living with his angle of vision focused upon life from the fourth and fifth dimension, and with his interest concentrated in life as it is expressed in radiations, vibrations and the interplay of energies, his mind will reason in numbers and symbols rather than in words. His communications with the lower kingdoms will develop this habit of thought, which to us seems terrible now. But to him radiations will express the living moving love of Christ, and numbers and symbols the Mind and the plans of Divinity. In those days a man's visiting-card will be his horoscope, which will be summed up by the recipient with the sole object of discovering and ministering to his particular need.

As Christ came to show us, service will be acknowledged as man's greatest privilege and destiny.

Even such high ideals, however, if seen through the lens of selfishness, can be distorted and misused. Naturally, un-balance, or 'sin', will continue to play handmaid to humanity's progress, or a static condition would ensue. Indeed, the more mental power that men gain, the more dangerous and dyna-mic will be that power if misused. They will no longer commit crude physical crimes, such as theft, rape and murder. Their sins will take a mental or radiatory form, and be the more far-reaching for that. The weapon of the controlled mind will become a terrible temptation to those who still harbour the germs of power-lust and personal ambition. They will be largely safeguarded by the fact that dissimulation will no longer be possible to any great extent among their highly sensitised companions. Thought-reading and telepathy will have become very prevalent gifts.

In measure as communication through and interpretation of numbers, symbols and radiations progress, and as the power of telepathy strengthens, so will the use of words decrease. The vast sea of repetitive and automatic conversation in which we are engulfed today will disappear with other wasteful horrors of these times. Words will be used sparingly and with power. As men develop their concentrated mental faculties the words they utter will automatically be imbued with force, and pro-ductive of strong chemical and electrical influences. This will ably be demonstrated by scientists, and the study of effects to be achieved by chanting, singing and rhythmic or poetic speaking will come to the fore. This growing science will be used for development, for healing, and for intercourse with non-human individualities.

One of the greatest events which our near ancestors will experience will be the wearing away of the subtle veil which now separates the so-called living from the so-called dead. Strangely enough, the result of this will not be a close communion between the two. People will learn to leave their departed connections in peace to pursue new tasks, gain new experiences and profit from a complete change and rest from earthly living. Only in certain cases and at certain times will those in the flesh work and communicate with their disembodied relatives and friends. This will mostly take place during sleep, and thus this much-abused occupation will be given its vital importance in men's lives.

However, when it becomes possible to establish genuine communication with those of the 'dead' who have escaped from the restrictions of human mentality, information of a much higher order than that which filters through today will help to broaden man's outlook on all personal matters. Particularly will the whole question of sex and marriage take on a new and startling aspect. Many secrets related to sex will come to light. They will provide the basis for a new modelling of social foundations, enabling the world to be remade from its very roots, and producing the final clue to the future science of living—the science of the GROUP.

PART IV
Dedication

20

The Mystery of the Group

Our glimpse into the future has led us very far ahead indeed. It may be asked what possible practical usefulness can come from the contemplation of circumstances infinitely removed from our present life. The answer to this is that in order correctly to establish one's direction it is necessary to visualise one's goal. The shorter the focus of this vision, and the nearer the goal, the more will time and attention be given to unessential details, and the more likelihood there is of being deflected from the path. But if the ultimate and true goal is kept always in view, much time and many experimental mistakes will be saved, and men will continually have the inspiration of grand achievement and wonderful destiny to sustain them.

Having pictured the coming chapter of humanity's existence in its broadest outlines, we can now approach nearer home and consider the first steps which will be taken in the building of the new civilisation. The fundamentals of any civilisation rest upon the conditions of social living, and upon the personal relationships existing between units of a community. Most people will say that the relationship of the sexes is the most powerful factor in the building up of the social framework. But sexual life has always been subordinated to existing social conceptions and taboos. So we must first consider the more vital of the coming changes in the life of the community, and then we will have ready the framework into which future sex relationships will have to fit.

In our contemplation of the human family we are going to seek to unravel the mystery of individuality; to find the pattern and the plan which underlies the medley of crowded, mixed and varied types, the apparently haphazard and inconsequent assortment which comprises the population; to determine why they are all so different and what these differences mean; and why, nevertheless, they fall into definite classifications—the stupid and the intelligent, the coarse and the refined, the followers and the leaders. We will inquire how these conditions can comply with the picture of true Christian socialism and of ultimate achievement for all men.

We shall attempt to solve this riddle and to show forth the coherent pattern upon which the whole human family is built, and which it will one day beautifully picture.

Where shall we look for a clue to this pattern?

Wise men of old looked at the stars. They held that the lesser is a mirror of the greater. The Macrocosm (universe) is the model for the Microcosm (man). Wise men of today look within the atom, reading there the same story. They see our solar system as a group of varied planets around a central sun. They see the atom as a group of electrons around a central sun. They see our solar system as one of a group of solar systems around a still greater sun. The pattern of the group around a leader builds the universe from atom to constellation.

The immutable laws which built creation and hold it in manifestation are known to us. They are pictured in our religions and they are demonstrated in our laboratories. The primal impulse of life, the One, the Creator, spoke the Word. This first and major vibration produced the initial pattern and the initial division into Two, the Father-Mother, positive and negative 'electricity', male and female, spirit and matter. Thus was the world built upon the fundamental law of love and of sex. Love came with the Son, the consciousness produced by attraction and interaction between spirit and matter. Thus we have the primal division of the Trinity. The process of division continued, the Three dividing into Seven, the seven great Energies imbuing matter, the Seven Spirits before the Throne, pouring Their forces through the seven major planets of the solar system. Thus we see the great pattern of life set up before us. We can conclude also that the initial division of positive and negative electricity shared in this process of redivision also, producing seven types of electricity, the discovery and understanding of which lies far ahead.

The scientist uncovers the same pattern in the world of atoms and elements, stating that in the beginning there were only two elements, two gases, Hydrogen and Helium, from which all the vast array of atoms came forth, built from the results of division and blending. He knows that the number of Seven governs his tables of elements and atoms to a certain degree, but it is not the only key-number.

Nor is Seven the completed cosmic number. It is the number which rules many aspects of *physical* life. But a more complete cosmic number is Twelve. For there are really twelve planets connected with this solar system, and the division of the heavens is into the twelve Signs of the Zodiac, ruled, according to esotericists, by the Twelve Hierarchies. From this great primal pattern, and by a process of subdivision, the universe was built into physical manifestation. The Twelve grouped around the Creator gives us the cosmic key-number of Thirteen. This design evidently gave the correct number and arrangement of complementary forces suitable for the wielding of power and the act of creation. Thus we see the pattern of potency and of completion set up before us. We see the social organisation of the hosts of heaven, the stellar bodies veiling stupendous individualities.

When Christ came to dwell among men, and set us a model of living, He pointed out the significance of the number thirteen by placing Himself at the head of twelve Disciples. We do not know the birth-dates of these Disciples but they are held to represent the Twelve Signs of the Zodiac, the twelve phases of cosmic and human development.[1] As such, they

[1] See *The Finding of the Third Eye*.

would each embody a different definite astrological type representing a certain admixture of planetary chemical and electrical forces—a reflection of that admixture or *alchemy* which goes to make one of the twelve divisions producing physical manifestation. If each of the Twelve divisions were represented in the person of a disciple, then the Twelve Disciples brought together as an integrated group would reproduce the alchemy of creation, and with their Spiritual Leader would represent in miniature the potent ingredients of creativity itself.

This scientific model which Christ set up for us as an example has yet to be understood and followed. The significance of what He did will only be brought home to us when the secret language of science is uncovered.

Christ showed us how to work with power, and though His material included illiterate fishermen and seemed a strange admixture, underlying it was the deep astrological knowledge which knew how thus to produce out of frail, faulty, but properly blended material, a power and a vibration which should outlive the centuries.

The divine division of the Two into Three, Seven and Twelve has, of course, always been known. But Christ demonstrated to us the significance, for us, of that last division, our nearest link with the creative pattern. This lesson was one of His greatest bequests to us, with its final symbol of the Last Supper, wherein even the Betrayer was included.

Christ taught the significance of the Group, of group-work and of group-strength, and gave us a working model of it. He implied that all men who were His followers were to do as He did, and more. Thus we see mirrored the pattern of a future Christian world. In the later chapters of evolution men will have come together in their natural groups, astrologically complete. Their capacity for working thus with potent mental powers, in ways which we could not now appreciate, will then be set in miniature model of the Divine Creator. Thus will men have attained to a fuller knowledge and a sharing of the Divine Mind Itself.

During the life of Christ, behind His group of twelve, stood the women. While the men were given the instruction and trained to be positively active, the women were always there, ministering unto them in their faith and silence. They were usually the first to perceive and to believe. They were the last at the Cross, and the first at the Resurrection. Whereas the male disciples represented the positive electrical aspect of spiritual living, the female disciples represented the negative hidden spiritual reservoir, the true anchor of action.

In producing the perfect unit of a human group there must be not only the correct planetary or Zodiacal representation, but also a workable balance between positive and negative, male and female aspects. These aspects are not represented by physical form alone, but may focus their power through the subtler parts of the individual.

All of these factors will be embraced by the scientific knowledge of the future, and their right application will bring unimaginable powers and experiences to mankind.

At present such groupings take place involuntarily or not at all. When a Prime Minister forms a War Cabinet today he is working blindfold and hampered by ignorance. If the Cabinet turns out to be a potent unit there has been an instinctive coming together of those whose egos will in the far future combine to form a dynamic astrologically perfect group.

As the sun of the new era slowly shows his rim above the horizon of present history we can see coming into growth around us the seeds of the new group-spirit. Since the beginning of this century groups have sprung up in ever-increasing profusion. They are immature, adolescent and faulty, but the new impulse is at work already throughout the ranks of humanity. Finally we are hearing talk of the most ambitious group of all—World Government. This will also be an infant body when it does appear, and will have to be nursed through adolescence for many generations. When it reaches adulthood and coming revelation, it also will be built upon scientific human alchemy, and represent the Twelve Creative Hierarchies and Signs of the Zodiac in miniature.

Humanity will gradually build itself up into the repeated pattern of groups within a group. It will be realised that through this means the ultimate fruition of individual character development throughout the ages is obtained. For although we will no longer see the isolation of any one ambitious powerful ego, because fusion and sharing with others will be the rule, yet actual individualisation will be more emphasised than ever, producing, as it will, correct manifestation and understanding of a given astrological force and expression. It is as well to press this point continually home, because fear of loss of identity seems to be the bugbear which prevents many people from facing the greater laws of life.

The coming into existence of real group living will have fascinating results. It will do away with much of the spiritual and personal loneliness from which many people now deeply suffer. For the bond which will exist between those who have come together, to fit into their true place in life's pattern in an astrological group, will be a bond existing in the highest dimensions, and therefore more profound and satisfying than any other family or social tie. Of course groups of potential disciples can contain several members from one family, but such double felicity will be rare for some time to come.

Sensitive people have always longed subconsciously to find their own group, without knowing for what they were longing. They have translated this yearning into familiar terms and imagined that they were seeking for their 'affinity'. But no one human being can satisfy and develop all the facets of another human being. Only their own spiritual group can do this, providing as it does miniature human channels to all aspects of the universe. Assuredly also the true mate of any person is most likely to be found, in time, within his spiritual group. The absorbed and self-sacrificing devotion which many sincere people like to give to their partner in marriage or to a certain member of their family or close friend, is in reality misdirected. It is really just that quality of humility and obedience which is man's rightful offering to the Creator and His Plan, as served and mirrored in his own group, of which the Creator's representative is its leader or teacher. Future spiritual groups will be modelled upon that of Christ and His Disciples, expressing the closely integrated love and brotherhood which He commanded.

Thus, group-living will ensure loss of loneliness, a completion of the love and friendship aspect in life, a definite and permanent goal, a fount of trusted instruction, loss of uncertainty and of confusion, and a great combination of strength upon which all the members may draw.

Within a completed group must always be found the Betrayer, because the Saturnian (or Satan) influence is a part of the whole. In immature groups the Betrayer, after causing havoc, will be cast out as a factor with which the members are incapable of dealing. But as the groups become more advanced their attitude and capacity will change. They will recognise that the 'evil' one among them is offering them the greatest service, the service of the test and the trial, without which none may progress. They will stand the test, and in thanks for the service they will identify themselves with the 'evil' member through that love which absorbs and shares. The 'evil' thus divided will become negligible, and the 'evil' one redeemed, through being so fused with his group, through their love, that good and evil are blended and lost in each other. If Christ's Disciples could so have acted with Judas there would have been no betrayal because Judas, through sharing his doubt and misunderstanding with his Zodiacal Group would have had it clarified and resolved.

The lesson of fusion as contained in the establishment of the divine group in social living will be one of the great landmarks of the new dispensation. All thinking men will be trained to consider life from the angle of the great group patterns. The student will see his goal ahead in three phases of group integration. The first phase will be to achieve mastery or mastership of his own person, of the group which is contained within his own organism. The cosmic pattern of sun and planets is repeated in his own body as centres of revolving force which produce heart and glands. Man's own solar system is closely affiliated with and in process of expressing the greater solar system, in terms of quality and function. As soon as man has been able completely to co-ordinate and rule the group within his own periphery, and has achieved a measure of personal mastership, he is ready to meet and enjoy the brotherhood of his own group, and the teaching of the Master of that group (or His representative). Thus man, after having *discipl*-ined his own body, becomes himself the disciple.

The third phase is reached when man achieves the quality of teacher on his own account, and becomes himself the head of a group. He then finds that many of his past associations and relationships had witnessed the gradual coming together of those who were to form his own group. Even deadly antagonisms and enmities had concealed the interactions of this development. Throughout many vicissitudes his group inevitably grows. He remains a member of his own spiritual group under his teacher, through whom he gradually contacts a higher group of which his teacher is a member, with a leader more advanced than himself. So the pattern builds up, there being a place awaiting every person of every grade of attainment. The design is there already, and the people are there. They have not yet acquired sufficient spiritual sensitivity to work consciously in this way, although many of them are linked subconsciously, and working superconsciously together at this time.

Thus future man's attitude will undergo a profound change to many aspects of life. He will feel peculiarly responsible towards his own body and his own disposition and will become eagerly disciplined. Every active relationship between himself and any other person will be a subject of keen speculation and consideration with him. He will willingly care for his words and actions. For his ambition will be a mighty one, although it will embody humility and service. He will see long vistas of glory ahead, embracing attainment not only of the mastership of men, but of planet, solar system, constellation, until his spiritual group has become a fellowship of Deities.

Thus we have looked into the mind and the conceptions of

the man and woman of the far future. How near they will be to truth we are not in a position to judge, so argument will be idle.

The mighty law of the group will apply also to nations, who, considered as individuals, zodiacally representative, will gradually be grouped, and will finally become nation-disciples, forming a great World-Group at the feet of One Who is to Come.

21

Sex and Marriage

Our next step will be to seek to discover how the new dispensation will affect that all-important question of the relationship between the sexes. We must remember that upon this aspect of life the same new influences will be impinging, working to break down the old habits of separatism and of possessiveness, as well as of concentration on the third-dimensional or physical aspect.

The changes which are to come about in sex relationships will, therefore, be just as revolutionary as those in other spheres. We must bear in mind that we are not simply considering the trend of evolution, which is a slow process. We are contemplating a great change-over into a new way of living together, the beginning of a new chapter in human history, and the closing of the old chapter which has lasted several thousand years. When people say 'Human nature cannot change' they are referring to this great passing epoch wherein the same major influence has ruled all the time. They are unaware that this is only one distinctive chapter in human development which is now about to close.

All over the world and throughout history there have existed in various tribes and communities a variety of conceptions and habits relating to sex and marriage. These, although so different, have seemed adequate to meet the needs of some particular community. But in the main they have been swamped and lost to sight beneath the major conceptions and influences which have ruled the West, the advance guard of the last epoch, and with which we are familiar.

We have already given an introductory consideration of the tantalising subject of male and female.[1] According to both religionist and scientist the motif of the sexes runs through all of life from the marriage of the atoms to the magnificent consummation of constellations. The primary division of the One into the Two marks the beginning of descent into matter, or the slowing down of vibrationary rates. As we have seen, the formation of the Trinity brings the Son to birth, representing consciousness, set up by the interaction between positive and negative (or active and receptive) energies. These are the initial steps towards creation.

When the span of world history is over all will return to whence they came. The many will be resolved back into the One, and in the last act of world history we shall find the Two once more. Two is, therefore, the nearest number to Divinity, and is reflected by humanity in mating. Three is the number which links matter with spirit. Humanity reflects it in parenthood. For long have human beings blindly and ignorantly prostituted their most divine privileges. The coming days of revelation will close that pitiable and difficult chapter.

Remarkable developments will come about in people's attitude towards sex. Some of these will appear directly to be brought about by changing social conditions. Nevertheless, inner spiritual awakening will be fundamentally responsible.

We have seen how future living conditions will become far more pleasant than those of today so that no longer will a stupefied and deficient population rush to sex for the imperfect comfort, forgetfulness and defeat of loneliness which it may bring them. People will come to share so many joys that their needs will subtly change. We have also seen how the development of individual creative arts and handicrafts will feed people's creative urge, giving the natural result of habitual continence. It is already accepted that the indulgence

[1] See *The Finding of the Third Eye.*

in absorbing sports and hobbies curbs and satisfies many cravings and impulses.

Human beings today are suffering grievously from a variety of moral, mental and physical deficiencies. Deficiencies create cravings. One craving creates another. In the desperate effort to satisfy these cravings one excess leads to another, and peace is never found.

The vision we have beheld of coming changes leading to a saner way of living will wipe out many of the causes of deficiency. The normal and satisfied human being thus produced will become as sane and natural in his physical living as is a healthy animal. He will learn to be conscious of his 'natural instincts', which will not allow him to over-eat, over-sleep, or over-indulge in any of the appetites. Thus from the aspect of material and physical living alone, the difficulties of sex, as we now know them, will come to be forgotten.

The second great affecting factor in this respect will be the inception of true group-life. When people begin to experience the fulfilment of living in or with their own astrological group they will enjoy such richness of friendship, of brotherhood, and of close soul-fellowship and integration, that marriage and family life will cease to fulfil the same need as it now does. At present marriages are wrecked because people have to stake all their hopes upon them. They unconsciously and ignorantly demand from a marriage with one person the fulfilment and interaction which they should be getting from their group and teacher—twelve varied types! Marriage often fails because all of a partner's subconscious desires for what he senses as his birthright are wrongly focused upon it. Disappointment ensues, the Betrayer enters in, and catastrophe arrives. In those fortunate cases when marriage within one's true group occurs it will be safeguarded and enriched, bringing a degree of happiness not possible now.

Such marriages as are successful today are so either for the reason that people's natural psychological needs have become dulled and atrophied, or because several members of an embryonic group come together as a family. In this case the variety of types and the astrological complementaries can already be discerned.

Those conceptions of life which are today labelled as esoteric will be held by increasing numbers in the future. This will come about through a growing clarity and force in thinking, and through much that will be revealed from the inner dimensions. The belief in reincarnation or successive births of the ego will be widely held, but in a less childish manner than that obtaining today. It will be believed that every ego is tested throughout the complete gamut of human experience; that each must know motherhood, fatherhood, failure and success, prominence and obscurity, pain and joy, wickedness and understanding, self-indulgence and self-discipline; and that this entails constantly changing relationships between those groups whose destiny is to develop together, as well as frequent changes of sex. Sometimes connections of this kind are very numerous. This is because the astrological group of twelve is always the core of a much larger grouping.

A man will, under these conditions, be able to consider that his wife may have stood to him as sister, father, tutor, or even enemy at a former epoch, and that he himself has not been free from feminine frailties. This understanding will draw the sexes together in closer sympathy, and 'sex antagonism' will no longer find a foothold. It will also destroy the barriers of inhibition which now exist between parents and children.

Marriage as an 'institution' will undergo profound changes. 'Whom God hath joined . . .' will no longer indicate those human beings who have *themselves* decided to marry under the roof of a church. It will be known that such faulty human impulses have little to do with Divine planning, and that although they sufficed for an ignorant and infant humanity, they are obsolete for a people reaching adulthood and becoming sensitive and aware of their inner divine nature, and the laws of astrological affinity which control their destiny.

Men will learn to develop an inner touchstone where mating is concerned. They will know that marriage with the true mate is a luxury seldom allowed along the stern path of potential discipleship. So they will take 'second-best' without illusion, and with the knowledge why and how to make the best of it. In a certain sense marriage will acquire less import-ance, 'marriage laws' will largely disappear, and the true mating will be expected as the reward of the far future.

However, as the all-absorbing interest of these mentally polarised people will be in the education and upbringing of the next generation, children will not suffer from these changing conditions. They will constitute an ever greater need and interest. Although the personal possessive attitude of parenthood will disappear, together with its lack of under-standing, an intense interest and comradeship will take its place, together with a type of love with which we are not yet familiar.

Curiously enough, the laxity and carelessness in sexual morals which obtain today are the first results of an inner revulsion from the restricting egotism and self-centredness which has ruled sex-life up to date. They denote also the first blind movements towards the coming changes.

The powers of telepathy and thought-reading, as they grow, will alter the relations between people very considerably. The mask which so many habitually wear, the picture of them-selves which they desire to present to the outside world and even to their own conscience, is known to us as the personality. This was derived from the Greek word 'persona', meaning 'mask'. The persona will begin to fail in its purpose as people become telepathic, and will cease to be developed to the extent which it now is. The personality has become, in some cases, quite a hard outer shell, made up of mannerisms, inhibi-tions, shynesses, rigid static ideas and dissimulations. So con-crete does such a shell become in the ether surrounding a person that radiations or impressions can neither pass in nor out. Such a personality has become a useless instrument to the striving soul within, which is cut off from growth and develop-ment, and from intelligent contact with its fellows. Such con-ditions render quite impossible the task of recognising and attracting the right mate, and allow for the gravest mistakes to be made, because they entirely prevent that flowing back and forth of radiations, that power of reaching out on those radiations and identifying oneself with another living creature which produces true understanding and sympathy. This radiation and identification with life holds the secret of the new Love which is coming into the world, the Love which is Christ. We can hardly understand it as yet, because it is *not* a personal love. It allows a person to quit his own personality and *become* the one or the thing beloved, sharing the other's restrictions, qualities and outlook.

Christ demonstrated this Love in many ways. He wept at the tomb of Lazarus. He, knowing immortality, aware of the little, fugitive evanescence of human suffering, yet wept, because He identified Himself with the pitiable ignorant grief of those around Him. When the sick came to be healed He identified Himself with them also, looked into their warped or sinful minds, and seeing there the cause of their disease, said : 'Go, and sin no more !' Or, seeing the growing spark of spirituality within, said : 'Thy faith hath made thee whole.' Often His powerful radiations broke the hard shell of some 'persona', and the true character was set free or 'converted'.

This power and sensitivity of radiation, the Christ-love, is the new quality coming to birth in mankind, which will establish the conscious link between Christ, men and the rest of creation, and make possible the 'Second Coming'. It will change and heighten the quality of love between men, and especially the love between man and wife. In a community where thought-reading is becoming habitual, the personality can no longer veil, and dissimulation is negated, it is obvious that the choosing of a marriage partner will lack the guesswork, uncertainty and mixed motives which ruin men's chances of happiness today. In a community where a person's visiting-card is his horoscope, hypocrisy will have little place. That ingenuous frankness about the self which has already appeared in somewhat crude form in the advance guard of the new race, on the continent of America, will be the average attitude. People will look upon their own faults, not as something to be ignored, denied and hidden, but as the signposts to their potential virtues.

With such conditions of frankness existing, especially within a group, people will be able to help each other enormously, and do powerful team-work. Especially will such candour enrich and beautify the marriage relationship, making possible a mental and spiritual intimacy and comradeship even between couples who are ill-suited and ill-matched from present standards. Today even 'affinities' may marry without consciously discovering each other deep buried beneath the shells of personality.

It may be thought that with the disappearance of personality much of the 'romance and mystery' of life will be lost too. The mystery here referred to applies, however, only to little 'etheric' obstructions veiling the reality of the tiny spiritual germs which we call human beings. The true mystery is attached to the individuality, which lies back of the personality and persists while the other changes. The real romance of life grows with every fraction of the Plan of Creation as it unveils before us, both in regard to ourselves and to the universe, and can always be ours irrespective of place or person. The sooner we can switch the focus of our vision from off our little personalities, the sooner shall we revel in the grandeurs of cosmic all-pervading romance and mystery.

We know that 'a sorrow shared is a sorrow halved, and a joy shared is a joy doubled'. But spiritual understanding shared brings a bliss which transcends all qualifications. This bliss will be the new quality entering into the average marriage of the future.

The man of those times will have explanations for many circumstances which the man of today cannot explain at all. He will not be dogmatic or intense about his conceptions, and personal matters will not have the same kind of interest for him that they do today. At present a man is hard put to it to reconcile some circumstances of his life with his religious conceptions. Possibly he may have had several wives and loved them all dearly. He is puzzled why this has been possible, and as to what the situation will be when he 'has to face them all on the other side'! He cannot even be sure which was his 'true mate'. He is quite at a loss.

In such a situation the man of future mentality would feel that he had been offering the relationship of a husband to several members of his own true group, possibly not one of whom was his ultimate soul-mate, but all of them his dearest and eternal friends, under which bond a temporary physical relationship was, although serving its purpose, purely incidental. Various other intense relationships would come in the same category.

The psychologists of the future will have acquired some fairly clear cut ideas as to the divisions which go to make up the complexities of human disposition. They will understand that a man has a coherent 'body', vehicle, or instrument of action and perception, for use in each of the dimensions. His physical body of the first three dimensions is, of course, the one with which we are the most familiar. Invisible, so far, to most of us, is his body or vehicle for use in the ethers, known to esotericists as his 'etheric counterpart', through which electrical messages and impressions of many types are sent, including those of pain, pleasure and the other physical sensations. This vehicle will be considered as also in the realm of the physical. His medium of expression in the fourth dimension of radiation, ranged in the class of vibrations which the esotericists term 'astral', is a very vital 'body', inhabited in the case of the unadvanced man by his emotions, and in the case of the advanced type by the activities and radiations of the awakened heart. Man's instrument in the fifth-dimensional realm, it will be considered, is his mind, which itself divides into two, the lower or concrete mind, and the higher or abstract mind. As we have said these two divisions are represented in the anterior and posterior lobes of the pituitary body, the gland at the root of the nose. The linking of these two aspects of the mind provides the channel between spiritual and physical knowledge, and is the place where animal, human and divine man meet.

Future psychologists will learn that these four-dimensional divisions in a human being are made to dovetail, interlock and integrate through being alternatively polarised, positive and negative. Therefore a person with a feminine (negative) body would have a positive etheric vehicle, a feminine 'astral' vehicle, and a masculine mind. On the other hand, a man would have a positive masculine physical body, a feminine etheric counterpart, a positive astral vehicle, and a feminine mind. A little thought will make this arrangement seem probable to us even now.

For instance, a man with a well-matured *mind* (not brain) shows feminine traits of poetry, romance and love of beauty, philosophy and the creative arts. A woman with a well-developed mind shows powerfully masculine traits such as courage and ruling-power. Great women in history are principally the ones who stand out by reason of these qualities, such as Queen Elizabeth I, Victoria, Catherine the Great, Jeanne d'Arc, and Florence Nightingale.

If this argument were false, then the vast company of illustrious thinkers and artists would have been women, not men. Women artists and poets in history are conspicuous by their minority when compared with those in male ranks. However, it is a little difficult to follow this argument without giving long consideration as to the exact meaning of positive and negative when applied to the mind. The division into 'positive' and 'negative' really means 'active' and 'receptive', the 'flow' and the 'reservoir'. The word 'negative' is a misnomer and should not be used in these cases.

The present-day inability of most men to understand that women have potentially masculine minds, and women's neglect and prostitution of this power, cause many human possibilities, especially those of marriage, to be abortive. They prevent the correct team-work between the sexes from taking place. Women's suffrage was born from the instinctive knowledge of this masculine factor within them, but being without future psychological knowledge they were muddled as to the issues, and sought to become masculine in those aspects of living where their femininity is the strongest!

In everything that pertains to 'solid matter' woman is feminine and needs protection, but her etheric vehicle is positive and strong. That is why women are better pain-bearers than men; have the strength to draw all the electrical substances and forces from the ether necessary to child-bearing; and are more successful in learning to see and to sense the impressions found in the ethers, as in some forms of mediumship, psychometry and clairvoyance.

On the other hand, a man is positively polarised in his emotional, heart or 'astral' life, and a woman 'negatively' so. Women's emotions are feminine, receptive, long-held, and badly controlled; they often let her down. Men's emotions propel action, are positive and intermittent (positive action is always intermittent) and aid and inspire him instead of controlling him.

Future analysts will make careful differentiation between the dimension in which ether-sensitivities function, and the dimensions in which the emotions and the mind function. This may sound involved, but it will be far clearer than the confused suppositions with which psycho-analysts struggle today. The fact that we possess alternatively polarised instruments or channels to each dimension shows how closely we will one day be able to integrate, both with the surrounding world, within ourselves, and with our chosen mate.

When men and women know these things they will be able to live in a beautiful complementary way. A man will protect a woman's vulnerable emotions with his own stronger ones. If he does not do so today, and lets her down, she sometimes prostitutes her masculine mind to her assistance, and becomes a hard 'gold-digger'! Conversely, a woman will protect the receptive orientation of a man's mind with her own surer and stronger one. Because she has not so far done so, men were defenceless from influences like those of Herr Hitler, and world disaster followed.

The subtle, powerful and beautifully designed relationship

between the sexes is, indeed, the true foundation of happy living individually and collectively, whether or not marriage is entailed. Its understanding will be an extremely important part of future adolescent education. Its practice will lay the foundation-stones of a new civilisation of supermen and superwomen.

22

Power—Our Experiment Completed

We have now finished our lightning survey of the future. We can begin to sum up the results of our Meditation and Contemplation and discover what we have achieved by it.

We began our approach along lines of scientific thinking, although they were unlabelled by orthodox scientific terms. From a purely rational and almost mathematical angle of vision, we proceeded to build up a picture of the universe, piercing through from outward manifestations and effects to inner powers and causes. Helped by logical reasoning and deduction we constructed our scaffolding, and then watched it come to life as a true edifice. We took the broadest and longest view possible of evolution, visioning its stages in periods of many thousand years, thus seeking to focus our viewpoint more nearly in the manner of Those Who planned it. Having sounded the note of our conceptions and inquiries, we held that vibration, steadily and persistently, with concentration and poise according to the methods of Meditation. We then wrote down the vision which we were drawing to us.

We have put down our impressions exactly as they came to us, and although we believe them to approximate to the truth, they must now stand or fall on their own merits, and on the merits of their readers.

Assuming that some of these readers are inclined to accept, as I do, this picture of the plan and the future of the universe, we will now summarise what we have learned, and from it deduce our implied course of action. Remember, our prime purpose was to discover the clue to the present state of world affairs, to uncover the secrets of the evolutionary process and to determine what should be men's next steps towards the refashioning of their world and the achievement of their destiny.

We have seen that creation is evolving through a process of transmutation. The heat of desire, aspiration or love, whether burning in an atom or a man, causes disintegration of the heavy vibrations of the lower dimensions, a raising of their tempo and key, and then transmutation into the scale of vibrations existing in a higher dimension. The higher the dimension, the more movement and the more power. Humanity as a whole is passing, at present, from under the rulership of the third dimension and the separatism associated with physical form, into the period ruled by the fourth dimension and the fusion associated with radiation and love.

We have seen that the crisis through which civilisation is now travailing denotes the passage from one great chapter of evolution into another in which the fundamentals are reversed, and the entire *motif* of life will be changed over! Therefore the present confusion and difficulty give no cause for wonder. This great change-over is the point where, in the parable, the Prodigal Son (humanity) turns to return to his Father, his source, the One. The descent into matter of the Spirit is now over, matter has responded, and the return journey has now to be made. The lowest materialism, both chemically and consciously, has been gone through, so now the process of transmutation can be speeded up.

The plan is clear before us to this degree. Humanity is to break free from the third dimension, live the fourth-dimensional life for a period, while training and preparing for the coming fifth-dimensional period—or, in other words, humanity is to break free of materialism, live the life of true Christian love, sharing the Heart of Deity, while preparing for a future of creative power and the sharing of the Mind of Deity.

What are the immediate prospects? The inevitable changes

which are already upon us will involve the breaking down of all barriers of all kinds throughout life, and the integration of all its aspects, racial, governmental, religious, scientific, social, into the gradual formation of one coherent, beautiful, symmetrical and powerful whole. If we bear this last sentence continually in mind it will afford us the clue to any aspects of the situation which come up.

We have seen that the great change-over will ultimately produce some form of World Government, of universal religion, of master science, of practical health control, and of education for world citizenship and for potential Group life and discipleship; and that finally religion, science and education will themselves fuse until they are no longer recognisable as separate units.

We have seen that the passage of human consciousness from the third to the fourth dimension will bring it into the realm where it can contact the Christ-life, and that herein lies hid the mystery of the 'Second Coming', and of the foundation of the Kingdom of Heaven upon earth.

May I digress for an instant to mention that Sir Ambrose Fleming once made the inspired suggestion that 'Heaven might possibly exist in the Fourth Dimension'! How encouraging it is that the time has come when a *scientist* dares to say a thing like that!

We have learnt that the greatest event of this new period will be the advent of the Group genius upon earth, the understanding and following of the model set us by Christ. People will have evolved to the stage where they recognise and join their true destined group, wherein they are all astrologically complementary, and form together a unit of potent creative power.

We have studied the mind of future man, and we have seen that all the factors mentioned above will have radically reversed his entire approach to life. Relieved of countless fears, inhibitions and other stultifying influences, a vast amount of vitality, time and resource will be set free, both individually and collectively, and the true spirit of creativity and aspiration inherent in man will come to life.

We have visioned the great changes which will be brought about by the action of the radiatory world upon human life and the human psyche, and how an extension of the five senses to the perception of higher vibrations will open up a new world to men's understanding, a world wherein they can share and exchange knowledge with the other kingdoms in nature.

We have seen many other wonderful things, all of which point to one fundamental difference which will appear in men's lives. I think this is best summed up in the word POWER. Energies, wasted hitherto, will be conserved; higher vibrations will be developed and wielded. Knowledge will grow. The right co-operation of the sexes will give added strength. Men will become *stronger* morally, mentally and physically. Finally, the controlled and concentrated mind will be used as an instrument to wield and change physical matter.

The adolescence of humanity with its terrible initiations will be forgotten. Human beings will stand self-acknowledged as potential units of creative divinity; welded together in the insoluble and eternal friendships of fellow-discipleship and astrological destiny; as embryonic solar systems spawned by their parent planets; able only as yet to glimpse the fringe of future possibilities; but freed for ever from the hard school of ignorance, materialism and isolation.

The assumption of potential Deity may appear presumptuous to those who forget that it has always found place in religious teachings. Observe how far we have progressed already! Are not human beings today in many ways almost little gods—even if stupid little gods—compared with their ancestors the cavemen of not so very long ago?

In my last book we began with describing lofty spiritual conceptions and brought them down to tally and dovetail with the findings of modern science. In the present chapters we have begun with practical scientific thinking, and it has led us through to dovetail with the same spiritual laws. The ultimate Diamond of Truth is identical, no matter through which of its facets one penetrates. Nevertheless, we kept to our scientific outlook for as long as we were able—which was until we came to study the mind of future man, and saw that it was a blend of religion, esotericism (or occultism) and science, and included a very broad conception of the principle of rebirth in other spheres and dimensions as well as on this planet.

We have seen that man's ultimate way of approach to divinity and to fulfilment will be through group formation, through finding and taking his place in the intricate Zodiacal pattern of the universe. It follows that if we wish to understand life we must understand the design which runs through it from constellation to atom. We must realise that the process of physical creation is that of crystallisation from the One of highest completest vibration into a series of rates of lower vibrations; by means of which the One manifests by becoming the centre of a group of forces which are expressed in physical form as sun and planets, protons and electrons, heart and glands, leader and group, evangelist and disciples. We must understand the different key-numbers which build up group forms and cohere all groups, the Two, Three, Seven and Twelve; and the place and purpose of every expression of a Zodiacal Sign, and the character of the Ray which flows through and from it.

Let us consider for a moment the twelve Zodiacal Signs around the Sun in relation to their reflection as a perfected group of twelve potential disciples around their leader. The twelve Signs are alternately positively and negatively polarised, one Ray and one Planet ruling two Signs, one of each. The human group will have positive and negative equally represented, usually by containing six men and six women, in pairs, each pair working for the aspect of life ruled by one particular Ray, its Planet, and its positive and negative Zodiacal Signs. These aspects may be stated as Power, Love, Intelligence, Harmony, Religion, Art and Organisation, although dozens of other terms are applicable to them. Power, of course, is the aspect of the Sun, the incarnate, or discarnate, leader, or the spiritual force behind the group.

In time World Government will take the form of such a group, which will be repeated at the head of all lesser organisations. Until such group formation is understood and put into practice, humanity will continue to suffer from the unbalanced judgments, ill-calculated administrations, and tyrannies which inevitably take place without it. A true group formation will always balance up one-sidedness and absorb and negate a power complex.

The world's beautiful music is built up from the group of twelve, the octave of seven white notes and five black ones, underlining still further the creative completeness of that number. As for colours, most of us are only able to see the initial seven of the rainbow, but those with extended visual perceptions see twelve colours.

When humanity has the intelligence to organise itself according to the models shown forth so plainly in nature, it will express in living the same harmonious fusion as we enjoy in melody and in the rainbow. The understanding and appreciation of these beautiful laws lies far in the future. It is the rare privilege of the pioneers alone of any age to sense things far ahead. The true pioneers of today will be those who, anticipating future developments such as we have outlined, have begun already to work towards those ends, thus inaugurating on earth the blue-print of the plans waiting poised in the fifth dimension. Too little is, as yet, understood of astrology for much to be done from that angle, although potential groups already exist, even if unorganised and unaware. When the right note is sounded many of them will be drawn together.

How should we recognise those pioneer spirits already in existence who can feel the call of fusion and integration?

A doctor of such a type would readily agree that he will learn more about healing if he consults with a 'pioneer' type of priest, a musician, an electrical scientist! An agriculturist of such a type would be ready to organise his work in conjunction with an economist, an astrologer, a dietician! A musician of such a type would consider collaborating with a psychologist, a colour-visionary, a perfume expert!

All those who have *grasped* the secret of the essential interplay and interdependence of all life will be ready to attempt to work in this way, and will expect to receive unique inspiration from so doing. They will not be disappointed.

During the passing period of separatism, before group work of the kind we have foretold could take place, any great creative output necessitating a 'Zodiacal', or complete, outlook on life, had to be achieved by one man alone, who therefore had to combine almost the whole group quality of expression within himself. The group genius had to incarnate in one man, future head of a group, thus producing a giant intellect and a character of many talents and facets who, in thus expressing a divine principle, showed forth in many cases the 'gifts of the Holy Ghost'. Such men usually drew to them their future group in embryo, in the guise of satellites or apprentices. Such groups would grow, obviously, through the process of reincarnating through both good and evil lives.

As examples we may mention Paracelsus, the 'prince of physicians', precursor of therapeutics, who introduced mineral baths, and was said to capture celestial rays in dew, invoke spirits and raise the dead; Roger Bacon, the all-round genius who reformed the calendar, and worked on lenses, spectacles, telescopes, gunpowder, flying-machines, microscopes and other scientific inventions in the Middle Ages, and was an astrologer, alchemist and magician; Democritus, the great philosopher and anatomist, and 'father of experimental science', who practised divination, prophecy and magical healing; Pythagoras, who gave us the laws of mathematics, astronomy, music, geometry, and much else, and who believed in rebirth and astrology and healed with music, colours and herbs; Wagner, with his stupendous cosmic conceptions and vision; Swedenborg, with his scientific genius, his art, his literature, and his mystical life and prophecies; Leonardo da Vinci, with his art, his engineering, his flying-machines and his magic; and Shakespeare, with his astonishing knowledge of magic, freemasonry, astrology and its expressed human types.

So many of these great representatives of future collective genius have shown forth those gifts which developed mental and spiritual powers bring. Of such are prevision, healing, wisdom in spiritual law, scientific knowledge, and an interest in the practices of alchemy and magic. When they have surrendered their stewardships to their ripening groups, those groups will collectively possess those powers and interests too.

Thus the ultimate World Government itself will possess collectively prevision, and an understanding of the divine plan.

In measure as men become able to respond to the group genius and to group work, so does the necessity for great solitary creative geniuses pass away. That is why those who have been the pioneers of the dying age of art and separatism need no longer stand out among men and bear the burden of publicity, but may retire to their rightful place behind, or within, the shelter of their maturing groups. Therefore the day of Michelangelos and Wagners is long over.

The outstanding men of these times belong in a different category. The next chapter of human development will see the learning of the wielding of mind-power, the *real* power. Many of the leaders of these future power groups are alive today and have begun their work. This work is still in primitive, in crude and seemingly ugly form, but it presages a great future. The use of power is dangerous and difficult for men to learn, so that is why it constitutes a later lesson than that of art or of love. Men begin the power lesson in the physical world, with the controlling of money, property and labour. Later they gain power over the emotional world. Both these phases are unstable. Finally they gain power by using 'hypnotism', or the mental rays, thus beginning to employ either 'black' or 'white' magic; one then sees the results of the development of the human power to draw upon cosmic forces. This latest innovation is powerful enough to upset the entire human family. It was the secret underlying the Hitler régime, and explains its extraordinary influence. The same new force had been slightly drawn upon in both Italy and Russia.

In the hands of amateurs, or of those with as yet un-
developed character and vision, it is a terrible and destructive
force. But let us look more deeply. In order to shatter the
thousands of separative barriers and form-shells of the dying
age, and let in the light and force of the new dispensation,
old forms, physical, etheric and mental, *must* be broken up,
and higher vibrations must be established through the heat
and stimulation of suffering and endeavour. Man must pay
his entrance fee into the wonderful future life of power.
Therefore those outstanding egos who are performing this ugly
task of destruction for humanity, and arousing the human
family in spite of themselves to true universal responsibility,
are contributing a great and thankless service. To do this
service some have forgone even their own spiritual life for a
time, and allied themselves with Saturnian work, passing with
their groups through a very purgatory. Let us not criticise in
horror their work of barbaric destruction, but rather be
ashamed that there has been found no other way to arouse us
all to a shouldering of true Christian responsibility. How incal-
culable a service is any which speeds up human destiny and
initiation.[1]

Let us pause, therefore, always when upon the brink of con-
demnation. Could we but pierce the veil of time and perceive
the eternal threads upon which certain big lives are strung,
how differently we might regard them.

Who were and are Mussolini, Hitler, Stalin? *Who* were,
and are, and will be, de Gaulle, Robert Kennedy, Nasser, the
Pope? What is the real status of these strongly individual
egos?

Such knowledge is of the future. Our first step should be to
realise that somewhere such knowledge does exist. Only such
acceptance will ever tune us in to the receiving of it.

All knowledge of this kind means Power. It means working
consciously in light and understanding instead of blindly in
darkness and through guesswork.

Beauty, love, power! Three stages of human development

[1] See *The Initiation of the World.*

on the pathway to divinity. The pagan and Grecian gods gave us beauty in the third dimension. The Buddha gave us the wisdom of the heart in the fourth dimension, and Christ gave us the love of the heart in the fourth dimension. We may expect One to come in the dim future Who will teach us the right use of the new force of mind-power in the fifth dimension. Until it is safely and faithfully controlled we must expect such abuses of it as were those of Hitler and Stalin. We cannot pass judgment upon them until we understand what a terrible *new* force is being offered to humanity to master.

It is this understanding which we can now achieve through having lifted the veil of time and visioned man's ultimate goal. This is to be the mastery of the fifth dimension, the attainment of mind-power, involving a changed life impossible for us to comprehend today. This destiny is not for the few, but for us all. It is terrifying but glorious. Humanity is still in the *chrysalis* stage. It will emerge into as different a life as does the dragonfly from its sheath.

23

Man the Magician—Summing Up

To perform magic entails the knowledge of just those secret laws of nature which we have been uncovering. It requires the understanding of the power which the higher vibrations possess to affect lower ones. It necessitates the capacity to use the instrument of highest vibrational potency in the world— the human mind, as a weapon of power, and controlling it with the will, to project rays and thought-patterns from it which will disintegrate and rearrange the atoms and their formations in the lower vibrations.

There are two kinds of magic, 'white' and 'black', or 'good' and 'evil'. Black magic is worked by those who have not yet escaped from separatism, and who are of the passing epoch, being ruled by personal ambition. This holds them down from using the vibrations of love and of mind in the upper dimensions. They are obliged to work with the vibrations and rays of 'animal magnetism' with those of the ethers, which still belong in the upper reaches of physical and form life. They do not work from the realm of causes, but interfere with effects.

White magic is produced by those with powerful minds who are inspired by an impersonal wish to serve and help, and to work in company with the forces of evolution. They affect the designs and patterns in the fifth dimension, producing profound changes from within outwards, and their power can be great and beneficial.

Men have achieved incredible scientific wonders without the use of magic or mind-rays at all but merely with brain-power. It can be imagined to what greater heights of achievement they will rise when their higher potentialities are allowed to come into play.

The law of progress decrees that each dimension must be conquered through the mastery of its own vibrations by its own vibrations. The human spirit has had to conquer physical matter with physical matter, with its own body and with physical instruments. This is the first step in evolution, and sets transmutation in motion. Man has been given the task of mastering the dimensions, one after the other, from the lowest upwards, in their *own* domain.

The conquest of the third dimension has necessitated the most terrible sacrifices for the human spirit, the submergence into the 'Dark Ages'; while in the lowest man has had to *be* of the lowest, cut off from his perceptions in higher dimensions, unaware of them, separated from his knowledge of survival, of reincarnation, of his own potentialities, and of his own soul which is Joy. Only his spirit, Will, was left to him in this struggle, which he has performed blindly, stubbornly, patiently and wonderfully. He is about to win his way out of it, having borne the burden of matter and raised it upon his own shoulders to transmutation.

His suffering and his tenacity have been supreme, and he has won through. The weary battle is nearly over, and he can look forward to new life and new work, as his next task comes into view. This will be the mastery of the fourth dimension in its own realm. This means the conquest of all things through Love, radiation and identification. It means the fusion of soul with body, the linking of man with Christ. It means the coming of joy into human life, calm, natural, permanent joy, very different from the artificially stimulated intermittent pleasures which we struggle for today. It means the loss of half our desires and needs, because they are fulfilled from within. It means true happiness, the happiness of those well content to strive and to suffer because of the glorious goal ahead. It means power, the power of partial freedom from the bodily shell and from the confines of time and space. It means magic, the use of the warm radiations of love, and the power to see and feel much that before was hidden.

The struggle to master these novel conditions will be a keen and difficult one. It will be a conscious struggle, without the blindness, despair and melancholy of the fight with matter. Its burden will be tension and exhaustion. Human beings will become like over-charged batteries. Not all of them, of course. Progress is never equalised, and folk focused in various dimensions must dwell together, as they already do. There will be many already matriculating, as it were, for the third epoch, the conquest of the fifth dimension. These will be the great magicians of the coming centuries, men with incredible powers, whose minds can unleash a force stronger than the smashing of many atoms. Such men have already lived, although rarely. We can call to mind the miracles of Moses as an example.

After men have matriculated to power in higher dimensions they will never lose their interest in all that pertains to physical life. The physical world has a peculiar and unique usefulness, which becomes more apparent with progress. It plays the part of whetstone to the knife of endeavour; of lever to the fulcrum of progress; of anchor for the world of spirit; of shadow in a world of light; it provides the material for the development of will, patience and creativity, for the growth of embryo deities. The beauty of the physical world is a reflection of Divinity, it is Divinity's hand-mirror. It may be loved by men because of this, and by Divinity too!

The present 'mechanical age' is man's mirror! It is the mirror of his own interior powers, and the return which physical matter offers him for his services. It is he, personally, who is the potential independent Flying-machine! Television! Telephone! Bomb! It is he personally who will eventually produce heat and light sufficient for his comfort. It is he who will consciously help to run the universe, and evolve the plan of creation.

How differently all of us will feel when we have earned the right to know what we are, and to perceive our destiny.

24

Ultimatum

Our experiment is now complete.

We have obtained a tentative picture of evolution, and of the plan and pattern upon which it is founded. There may, and will be, errors of detail in our picture, our inexperienced vision is bound to have a more or less blurred focus. Conviction is strong, however, regarding the main issues of our vision of the future, which tallies also with the teachings of orthodox and of mystic sciences, both of past and present, welding the two together harmoniously. Further vision may come later, but we have now quite enough to set to work upon.

The law is: 'Until you have spread knowledge acquired, and acted upon it, the channel remains closed to the entrance of further inspiration'.

The next stage for us is action.

What must we do, all those of us who accept the plan and purpose of life to be approximately as here portrayed? We must bear continually in mind the implications of our discoveries, we must approach and regard all developments in the light of our prophetic vision. We shall now be able to discriminate between those people and activities which are trending in the right direction, and those which are still clinging to outworn forms and ideas. We shall know where to place our encouragement and our energies. Our attitude to life will be more definite and constructive. We can each in our own particular niche set up a growing fourth-dimensional viewpoint and radiation, becoming little lighthouses guarding and emanating the influences of the future.

Before we can thus radiate, this vibration must be firmly established within ourselves—we must get the picture clear, keep it so, and *live* it. We will then sound a creative note out into the universe, the power and effect of which will be commensurate with the strength of our own convictions. Faith the size of a grain of mustard-seed can move mountains. One man with utter conviction can deeply affect the world.

To *be* is to become. If we are thinking and feeling aright, good action will automatically follow, the requisite magnetism will inevitably flow from us, and the necessary people will be drawn towards it. It does not matter where we are nor what is our occupation. Power works in the upper dimensions irrespective of objective circumstances. We can be as potent an influence whether we are organising a big movement or digging in a backyard allotment.

Let us first make this great truth our own. To do and to become we must first *be*. There must be a sun before it can shine. This state of right being must first irradiate and inspire ourselves, making of us the perfect instrument. Secondly, it must irradiate our immediate surroundings, creating harmony and understanding between ourselves and everyone in touch with us; there should be no wish to change other people, but rather the capacity to accept and appreciate them just as they are, recognising always their latent divine potentialities, which will flower in their own good time.

As soon as we are aware of, and in the act of, establishing these first two stages, then only are we ready safely to step out and help to put the world in order. For to establish fusion one must oneself be completely fusible! To establish the life of impersonal love upon earth one must at least have a glimmer of what it is like! Once we are tuned to the right chord within ourselves our whole beings will be flooded with divine melody, and the song of evolution will be clear in our ears. Once we have firmly linked ourselves with the fourth dimension, with the Christ-life, with our own souls, we will vibrate with joy, a joy which informs and illumines all suffering and difficulty upon earth.

Let us remember that soul *is* joy, the reflection of Spirit which is Bliss. The surest test of our link with the soul in the fourth dimension lies in the existence within us of an eternal note of joy, sounding steadily throughout all our earthly dilemmas, pains and tortures. Those who have achieved this link can testify that it is so. Joy is what this poor world needs. Its loss has been the greatest tribulation and sacrifice attendant on man's submergence in matter.

So, firstly, let those of us who would rebuild bring joy, the soul radiation, into our environment. This must be the foundation of our edifice.

Secondly, let us bring unity. Let us find each other. Let us link up, and pool our resources of inspiration, wisdom, strength, purpose and conviction. We shall soon discover that we are sounding a note strong enough to rally both the seen and the unseen to endeavour. This endeavour will be nothing less, in the last analysis, than to prepare the way for the 'Second Coming', to give that particular offering which will enable the 'Kingdom of Heaven' to emerge on earth. Those are no longer beautiful and meaningless words—in these chapters we have filled in the picture, and brought them to life.

Thirdly, let us be practical. We have the blue-print before us. We see that it is planned upon the law of synthesis, the blending of all facets and activities of life, the formation of groups, each representing all-round complete links with human living. There can no longer be purely scientific groups, or occult groups, or political groups or artistic groups. Each group must possess a channel and a link to all of these. The structure for the new civilisation must be planned by such integrated representative groups as these. This is the quickest and the only way to world liberation. Potential members of these groups move among us today. They must be recognised and linked together. The 'army of the new dispensation' must be mobilised. Remember that war and its propaganda is the 'vice' side of an equally strong complementary virtue, the virtue of mobilised faith and light, the propaganda of wisdom, the force of love, and the power of high endeavour, all of which becomes irresistible if allied to the strength of plan, purpose and organisation.

Fourthly, comes organisation. Let us not fear it. From Deity downwards the whole universe is thoroughly organised, the keynote being always the keeping of balance between all facets of existence, a balance, however, in which one aspect always slightly predominates. In the atom the predominating side is that of the 'positive electricity'. In human living it must also be the 'positive electricity' which is in reality the reflection of the spiritual element. It is to be hoped that when pioneer spirits are linked together in this way they will lay the foundations of future group-work, building up a central radiation and a plan of procedure and collaboration, so that those foolproof projects for world order throughout all branches of living, for which we are waiting, will be steadily brought into being.

When in this manner the advanced intellectuals of the world come together to meditate in unison, what power and what inspiration will be released, what vision will be experienced, and what work will be achieved! For something new will have happened. The human family as a whole will have achieved an integrated intellect!

The human being depends upon his mind for rational and successful living. The entire human family is also one being— but it is still scatterbrained. Our lunatic world must have a collective mind, sufficiently powerful to influence it, before present madness can end.

The task that lies ahead for those who will embrace it is to

GIVE THE WORLD A MIND!